Barbara Lamont

City People

MACMILLAN PUBLISHING CO., INC.
New York

COLLIER MACMILLAN PUBLISHERS
London

Macmillan Publishing Co., Inc.
866 Third Avenue, New York, N.Y. 10022
Collier-Macmillan Canada Ltd.

Library of Congress Cataloging in Publication Data

Lamont, Barbara.
    City people.

        1. New York (City)—Social conditions. 2.
Lamont, Barbara. I. Title.
F128.52.L286   309.1′747′104   74-31141
ISBN 0-02-567690-3

FIRST PRINTING 1975

Printed in the United States of America

To Ludwig, David, Lisa, Michel, Mom, and Herb—and to all my fellow straphangers who, seeing that I was working, kindly refrained from stepping on my toes, joggling my elbow, or pinching my posterior.

ACKNOWLEDGMENTS

The author wishes to extend her thanks to Westinghouse Broadcasting Co., Inc. for permission to use material from the following programs she originally broadcast over WINS Radio in New York: senior citizens series, S.R.O. series, Co-op City series, Haiti series, addicted veterans, Indian power, Model Cities (Brooklyn), Model Cities (Bronx), drugs and crime, Dannemora, Bronx crosses series; and to Metromedia, Inc. for permission to use material from the Haiti series, the addicted veterans program, and the Model Cities (Brooklyn) program, all originally broadcast over WNEW-TV New York.

Contents

PROLOGUE

It was the pink terrace that made us decide to take the tiny brownstone apartment—separate bedroom, one-fifty a month on West End Avenue. We planted watermelon vines, tomatoes, and five-foot sunflowers that grew until there was barely room on the terrace to stretch out with a glass of lemonade or milk. I had just turned nineteen, and shortly after we moved in I went away to sing, to make money, and feel important in my fourth month of pregnancy. When I returned after eight weeks, creeping vines had turned the terrace into a little jungle, and the shuttered apartment with which we shared the terrace was rented.

Her name was Terry. She wrote words and music, played the piano softly, and smiled shyly. He was a Berliner Jew who was fond of stroking her hair and back. They gave the air of being new with each other, although

3

*it was hard to tell, as they had an aura of great privacy
about them; you couldn't just jump over the terrace wall
without a yoohoo.*

*He was a car salesman who always had ready cash and
let it be known that he had been a big black market trader
during The War. They were ten years older than we, and
she had a slender daughter, Brenda, who had her mother's
shy smile and talked with me at length across the terrace
about interracial marriage and life in general and important things, the way you do when you're eleven and unsure.*

*She had just gotten used to calling him daddy. We called
him Dory. I used to nurse my new baby on our pink terrace, and we would talk about Vienna, Rochester, the
future. One day the four of us went to see about buying
into a new brownstone co-op being built a few blocks
away. We couldn't afford it just yet, and Dory and Terry
decided not to live in a building where they would know
everyone and where everyone would know them. It was
the only time we ever met in the street, off the terrace.*

*I left for Europe when the baby was five months old
and never lived in that apartment again. During my absence we sublet to a couple of hookers, one of whom tried
to jump off our pink terrace after a party one night. Dory
later told me they were very loud besides. They stole my
record player and my pink portable typewriter and my
pink clock radio, but left the pink bedspread. When I returned from Europe we moved in with Mother; Dory and
Terry had moved to Park West Village, a new moderate-
income development with trees and eighty-two small
green-and-white terraces.*

*We met again in front of Macy's five years later, after
my second son was born. She said her name was now
Anne, and she wore a beautiful black mink jacket with a*

diamond choker nestled against her copper skin. She no longer wrote music, but had become his bookkeeper, a more important position.

Three years after that I saw Brenda in the lobby of the Statler Hilton. She was on her way to a dance and was going to be married to a man twice her age. She still looked eleven and talked about her "boyfriend" in a worldly way that seemed somehow obscene.

Terry called me once about a benefit for sickle cell anemia. We invited them over one Sunday, but at the last minute they couldn't make it. We dropped by one evening with the kids. Dory and Terry wore pajamas and were cheerful. Even in a robe she was refined. Business was good, Dory told us; some time afterwards he sent us a card proudly announcing the opening of his own car agency.

And then, late one night, someone they knew and had let in to the apartment bound their hands and feet with masking tape and slit their throats. They were the only couple I know who would have died for each other.

I don't have a terrace or sing or nurse my three children any more, and my bedroom is blue. I stand naked in front of the mirror asking myself, what can I wear to a funeral that I can also wear on an undercover investigation of a housing project that I can also wear to my analyst that I can also wear in front of my station manager that I can also wear to dinner at the One Hundred Sixteenth Street Mosque?

As a radio and television journalist I am paid to inquire into and describe the turmoil of people who live in cities. The radio or TV set is not just a magnifying glass that brings our jungle existence into our homes in close-up focus; it serves as a two-way mirror. Each news story presents an image or view to the public, and if the story is well done, it reflects the viewer's own image right back at him. The viewers and I feel our own complex joys and anxieties in the stories of others.

If a wino urinates on my cameraman's feet, the smell will permeate the picture because the viewer will supply that smell from his or her own sensory experience. There was one story on addicted newborns that I filmed for three hours, edited, and transferred to videotape, and then couldn't bear to watch that night, because there on the TV screen you could virtually smell the talcum powder on the twitching baby.

All news media serve as conduits for the sharing of each others' good times and tragedies. They warn us of the pitfalls that surround our lives and work, and help us to cope with a day-to-day existence by showing us how others in the same boat are also coping. Unlike newspapers, radio and television present us with a crash course in life, complete with sound, music, color, and lights, only minus the four-letter words.

For several years now I have gone out on the streets six of every seven days and talked to people—old people, young people, black people, neglected people, loved people, family people, lonely people—about their problems. This is the story of where I went and what I found. It is also the story of how people showed me their lives and how I reacted to them, the story behind the facts, which although never broadcast, helps to evoke a response from listeners and viewers. Specifically, it is the paradox of many different kinds of people caught in the squeeze of urban life, traveling like Gulliver in the eye of the storm, expecting at any unexpected moment to be squashed. Exaggerating their ethnic, sexual, and economic differences, yet caught up in identical day-to-day problems of paying the rent, providing food, and raising children, they fight each other to the end, proving once again that only the fittest survive.

PART I

PART 1

A group of people pretending to be children stands on a country road and sets up a barricade. A car traveling rather too quickly comes down the road, a lone driver, a British soldier, at the wheel. He sees the barricade a fraction too late and, trying to swerve, hits it broadside. As the car rocks to a halt, the soldier climbs out, swearing. One rock hits his shoulder, another his arm, as the people pretending to be children rush toward him.

Clawing, drawing blood, pelting with rocks, stones, and branches, they finish him off. Kicking, stamping, stoning, shrieking, and wailing, they advance when other cars appear on the scene. An ambulance is brought up, but they defend their position, refusing to let the medics take the dead body.

The people pretending to be grownups are forced to re-

treat. One soldier later says he didn't use rubber bullets on them but would like to thrash their parents to death. The people pretending to be children never had any parents. They were born out of the womb of Revolution, on a kitchen table somewhere, with a bayonet cutting the umbilical cord and a team of raiders for midwives. And it is their successful pretense at being children that has once again saved their lives.

Four Walls Do Oft
a Prison Make

In some cities apartment ads in the newspaper read, "No Pets or Children. Single People Only." But in New York City, housing for single people is in short supply. Single room occupancy housing was originally created in response to the critical housing shortage after World War II. Large apartments were subdivided into six and eight single rooms; bathrooms and kitchens began to be shared. Although single rooms originally were rented to students and returning servicemen, in the nineteen-fifties they came to house large families of oriental or Puerto Rican immigrants. Now they serve a mixed population of working poor and welfare recipients, including a large block of problem-laden single people: the mentally and physically disabled, alcoholics, drug addicts, and the aged.

People who live in single room occupancy houses and

hotels share a bath with five or more other people, cook their meals on two-burner hot plates, and often have to walk up four or five flights to their rooms, where they may have only a single hook to hang their clothes on. The average room is eight to ten feet square with a small window. A chair, bed, and table are standard furnishings. Youngsters under sixteen are not supposed to live in these buildings.

Conditions in SRO houses began to worsen as maintenance costs rose and rent control was done away with. And as the general housing shortage in the city grew, the squeeze tightened even more on housing for singles. The city-wide crime rate soared, and residents of SRO houses became easy prey for break-ins, muggings, and more serious crimes. The mayor's office would periodically announce a "crackdown" on these dwellings, more popularly known as welfare hotels, but part of the problem was the great confusion in determining the different categories of SROs.

Close to two hundred thousand rental units are available for single room occupancy, licensed by New York City under a variety of conditions, and designated as rooming houses, lodging houses, SRO houses, and SRO hotels. There are more than seven thousand legal rooming houses in the city. A rooming house is a five or six-story brownstone used originally by one or two families, on which no overall renovation has been done; rooms have simply been rented out individually. There is usually one bathroom to a floor, and under the law not more than five tenants may share one toilet.

Then there are lodging houses like the ones down on the Bowery run for alcoholics and derelicts. They provide cubicles approximately six by eight feet in size, with only a bed, and charge a minimal daily fee of fifty cents or so. Meals are also available in some of these lodging houses, which see more than six thousand men come through their doors each year.

In another category is the single room occupancy house, of which there are about five hundred in the city. An SRO house consists of what used to be apartments; the only remodeling that has been done is the placement of locks on the doors of the rooms. The average SRO house is a large apartment house that has three hundred or more rooms, with the same requirement of not more than five tenants to a toilet, a standard that is not always enforced.

In a fourth category are SRO hotels. These have no limitations on how many tenants can use one bath. They are simply small hotels with no private baths. No count is kept of them because they are licensed under the category general hotel. It is thus impossible to tell from the license whether the hotel is an SRO or the Waldorf.

This flood of information on single room dwellings is not the outpouring of a vast store of knowledge in my head. It is the result of an intensive investigative report which began with a letter I got from a listener who said he was eighty-one years old. He begged me to "just come on down and take a look at the place I live in." The tone of the letter was eloquent, and so pathetic that I took it to my editor and asked for a night shift to go downtown and investigate further at a time when the writer said he'd be home. The letter was unsigned, but hinted that if I showed up at the right address I would have no trouble locating the author. Normally I wouldn't touch such a story with a ten-foot pole, but I hadn't gotten on the wrong side of anyone recently, and there was a ring of authenticity in the two pages scrawled on white, lined paper.

So one Tuesday around five-thirty in the evening I found myself in front of the five-story brownstone at 21 East Twenty-first Street. The narrow building, sandwiched between a barber shop and a larger commercial building, was in the middle of a quiet, dark block, one on which, even in the daytime, few children would be seen. A tiny sign out front pronounced it a hotel.

As the front door was unlocked, I wandered in. I had been nosing around for a few minutes when a little old man emerged who said he was the superintendent. It was a little awkward, as I didn't have the name of the person I wanted to see: so I introduced myself and began to ask general questions about the age of the house. I couldn't tell whether the super was on the side of the tenants or the landlord, but just as I started to say that I'd gotten a letter, another old man wandered in and waggled his eyebrows at me. Although I was confused, I sensed that someone, somehow, had expected me to call. After beating around the bush for ten minutes or so, I got out my tape recorder and asked if I could talk to the two of them together. The super led the way back to a dingy office piled with crates, pointing out hazards along the way.

"The elevator hasn't worked since September," he told me. "The only pay phone was ripped out of the wall six months ago and never replaced, and in case of a fire we'd all be trapped." He pointed out a locked exit door leading from the fire escape. But although the wall and ceilings were peeling, the hall and stairs seemed to be reasonably clean.

"I'm going to retire in six months and go live in Miami," said the super, settling himself among the crates. "I was born in New York and never thought I'd say that."

"Why?" I asked cautiously.

"Well, I've lost my respect for an awful lot of people in this town, and in these rooming houses especially. How do they behave?" He answered his question himself. "Wait until their checks come on the sixteenth or the thirtieth, and you'll find out how they behave."

"What happens?" I wanted to know.

"Well, everybody isn't the same. But what sort of people have you got that take their City checks and stay in their rooms all day and sleep and don't work? What New York City ought to do is give out a little more backbone to these people instead of money. If you were a man who had retired, or a retired seaman, or if you were a sick person that can't go out to work, or absolutely disabled, I could see it. But ˙they're not absolutely disabled; they move around. There are quite a few that are able to work, but since the City is good enough to pay the money, why should they?"

During this tirade the second old gentleman kept quiet, interjecting only a few comments from time to time. Suddenly he stood up and invited me up to his room for a cup of tea, in italics, waggling his eyebrows more obviously now behind the super's back. So I padded softly along behind him in my sneakers, up the stairs to the third floor, where he peered around quickly and then unlocked the door.

The room was miniscule, but he steered me to a rocker, then sat on the bed and switched on the radio.

"I stay tuned to WINS," he confided, "and when I don't want no one to hear what I'm saying, I turn it up real loud." He suited action to words, and then winked at me. "I was expecting you. I'm the one what wrote you, but you gotta promise not to use my name." I nodded in amazement, looking around the small room. There were at least fifty clippings pasted on the wall, as well as photographs and drawings of some of the first military aircraft. The old man explained that he was a decorated veteran of World War I, who had lived a few blocks away in Gramercy Park for twenty years after his retirement, but had moved into this hotel twelve years ago.

"One night in my old place, the doorman told me that I'd have to walk up for three months while they put in a self-service elevator," he sighed. "Well, I lived on the eighth floor; so I moved the next morning. I'd just come down the street and seen there was a place here that had rooms to rent, and I came in, and I've been here ever since. At that time there was a very fine class of people in this building," he told me in a frail voice. "And the owner was a specially very careful woman, very intelligent and very scrupulous. She didn't let anybody in the building unless she liked your looks. And you had to *be* yourself, not only look it!"

But, said the old man, morale in this new building had gradually declined, along with the services, when the building changed hands.

"The stairways used to be washed every morning," he said. "They haven't been washed since this building has been taken over. The elevator, if it was out of order at nine o'clock, by twelve o'clock it would be repaired, because the woman had a very fine credit. She employed only people that were serious in their work, and they did very good work for her, because she not only paid them but she always give them a gratuity."

The old man made two cups of tea for us on a two-burner hot plate, and we talked about the first World War and our mutual interest in airplanes. He invited me to walk around the building and talk to some of the other tenants.

As I walked down the hall to take a look at the common bathroom, I rather furtively changed cassettes in my tape recorder, tucking the used cassette down in a pocket, very much aware that I was on private property and could be forcibly ejected or otherwise threatened at any moment by the burly types passing up and down the stairs. The bathrooms were leaky, but not too filthy. The old gentleman introduced me to another single man, and we went into the latter's room, where he pointed out a leaky ceiling from which plaster debris had been falling for more than a year.

"Have you reported it to the landlord?" I wanted to know.

"Yeah, they all know it, but the guy downstairs, he doesn't care," he said.

"What did the landlord say to you when you told him about this?"

"I didn't see him," he said.

"You mean this has been going on for a year and you haven't been able to talk to him?"

"Uh huh. You can't catch them, they come in and they hide and then they leave." He shrugged disgustedly. He explained that he had been in a mental hospital and upon release hadn't been able to find another place to live.

"I'm on welfare," he said, "and I go back for treatment once a week." Talking to him, I got the feeling that he wasn't sure which was the outside world, the hospital or the rooming-house-go-round.

On my way out, as I passed a closed door, I heard loud Latin dance music. I decided to knock and find out if these were some of the types the super had complained about who lie in bed and collect welfare checks. I knocked on the door and the music was turned off. A rather stocky, bare-chested young man with dark curly hair opened the door and peered out.

"Hi!" I smiled brightly. "I'm Barbara Lamont from WINS Radio and I wonder if I could talk to you about what it's like living here?" From the way he looked at me I could tell I'd interrupted some serious action, but he was friendly enough.

"Maria!" he called. "Put something on." We went inside. A double bed was crammed into the small room, a radio stood on an orange crate, and one straight-backed chair was wedged into a corner.

"We're just waiting to get into public housing," said the man. His wife, a young, pretty, dark-haired girl of about eighteen or nineteen, nodded shyly. "We want to have children, and no kids are allowed here, so we try to get into the project, a nice one."

"Somebody might say 'what the hell, what are you doing in this hole?' " he continued. "I'm here because it's a hassle out there with an apartment, and to me this is a more decent place. The block, the people that I see around the neighborhood. Where I'm at, I'm in a better place than living in an apartment house maybe in another place where you know, some kind of different things are going on. You know, you buy a TV, and the next week it's gone. The only bad thing," he told me, his face darkening, "is I have to escort my wife to the bathroom. These filthy pigs, they stuff it up with grease and forget to flush it, and sometimes the lock is broken and they walk right in while you're taking a bath. So I stand outside the door when she has to go."

I thanked them and left, and the Latin beat was turned back up. Later, when I tried to contact the landlord at home to ask about the broken fire door, elevator, and phone, he refused to talk to me on the phone, saying he'd be glad to grant an interview in person. But when pressed, he concluded that he really didn't have time to do this either.

In the meantime the City had initiated a welfare hotel cleanup drive with six target sites chosen by the mayor for special efforts. These six hotels had the highest crime rate and the worst living conditions. Politicians were putting pressure on the mayor either to close the buildings, which they termed neighborhood centers of crime, or to go after their owners, using provisions of the criminal law.

One cold, rainy night as I was sitting in the newsroom trying to put together the story of the little building down on East Twenty-first Street, I saw a television news report in which the reporter was interviewing residents of one of the six bad buildings, a house on One hundred second Street. The camera followed him as he ran up the stoop and collared a tenant.

"Are you on methadone?" He wanted to know. From there the whole interview went downhill; the reporter stood at arm's length and the only questions he asked concerned drugs or how many crimes the man he was interviewing had committed. The subject blinked, mumbled, and finally ran off into the gloomy hallway beyond the range of the camera. The interview was so flaky that I got mad and stalked out, jamming a rainhat on my head and turning up my collar, and got on the nearest bus with my tape recorder tucked safely in an oversized shoulder bag.

I got off at One Hundred Second Street and started to walk down the dark block, not really knowing how to pro-

ceed. It was about 8:30 PM, and the block was already
deserted. So I simply stood there, looking up at the notori-
ous numbers nine, eleven, and thirteen.

A few days earlier number nine had been the scene of a
shooting in which a policeman was wounded and a young
woman killed when the police stormed in, allegedly search-
ing for a bail jumper. This building, famous as far away as
Vietnam for being a shooting gallery for heroin addicts,
has a long history. In 1970 police made over three hundred
arrests within a nine-month period in the six-story tene-
ment, mostly for drug abuse. One police commander told
me outright that he had stopped making arrests there because, after a brief appearance in court, the suspects were
back on the street before his men could return to the
precinct.

So there I was, standing in the drizzle, when a pair of
fourteen-year-olds came down the steps.

"Who you looking for?" they inquired.

"You live here?" I responded.

"No, I just visitin' my aunt," said the taller of the two.

"I'm a reporter," I said. "Do you think the folks who
live here would mind if I just started rapping on doors and
talking about living conditions?"

They giggled—"Where the cameras and lights?" I took
a long time to explain that I was a radio reporter, and
sure enough, by the time I finished my spiel, five or six
other people had gathered to listen in.

"I'm not here to ask if you all are on meth," I explained, "or to find out how many times you've been
busted, I just got kind of mad watching you get ripped off
on TV while I've got two million listeners who don't really
know who you are or what it's like living here."

"Have you got rats and roaches?" I turned to the larger
audience, turning on my tape recorder.

"Have we, honey!" shrieked one oversized character of indeterminate sex, who was leaning on the stoop.

"Look," I said, getting down to business. "I know about the crackdown and all the TV cameras making you look like shit. But all I want to talk about is not your personal business, but your relationship with the landlord. How do you live? Is it clean, do you get linens? Can you cook? How much do you pay each week?"

I had them hooked. What tenant can resist talking about his living conditions? They showed me into the small vestibule and really started rapping with each other, just twenty or so ordinary people. Some were older, but the majority were between the ages of twenty and thirty-five; some were mentally retarded, some were disabled vets, ex-cons, epileptics, undoubtedly some addicts; most were people who needed public assistance, who had just gotten out of the hospital or been enrolled in a methadone program. Their real story as I saw it was not so much their past experiences, but what conditions they were forced to live under on One Hundred Second Street.

"They say that so many people in here are selling drugs and whatnot," said a thin, wiry guy, one of the first to speak up. "I've been here for a year and the cops hasn't found fifty bags of drugs since I've been here, and that's a year."

"Ah, all the trouble comes from the people that comes in from outside, the people who don't live in the building," explained a woman. "Yeah, the people that got shot the other day, they didn't even live in here. They might have came to see somebody, but I'm tellin' you they didn't live inside the building." Everyone seemed to agree.

"Most everybody here is on a program," said another man, warming to his subject. To get on welfare, you have to be on a program for drug addicts, ex-drug addicts. But most of the people you hear about on the news, the ones that cause the trouble, they just happen to come in the building to see somebody or to hang around it because it's an open building with no lock on the door. Plus they go in there to hang out, out of the cold. They can't go in the Project where they have a lock on the door."

"How many baths are there to a building?" I asked.

"As far as taking a bath is concerned," chimed in the large person of indeterminate sex I had noticed earlier, "you can't take a bath, you know, because the bathroom's all messed up."

"What do you mean?" I asked.

"Nasty, you know. I mean peoples coming in naked and all that. There's no lock on the bathroom, you dig? So when people, just anyone off the street comes in, you know; I mean they just do what they want to do, and leave it like that. I used to try and clean it up, you know what I mean, but clean it up and the same thing will happen again. You can't even use the bathtub. If you want to wash, you got to buy you a pail, you know, and do it in your room." The people in the crowd nodded approvingly.

"How many people share a bathroom?" I wanted to know.

"Oh, everybody on the floor, ten or twelve of us."

An older man added that junkies come in and use the bathrooms as shooting galleries, to "get off" on heroin. "These guys from off the street, they be getting off, you know what I mean, they come up there and do what they want to then go back in the Project you know, wherever they live at, they do their dirt here and then they leave. And we the ones that's gotta suffer behind it."

"These used to be apartments?" I asked a young man who had just joined the group.

"Yeah, that was it; they're supposed to be roomin' houses, like. Most of us have one room, and then others have two rooms in one. "We got together and paid for locks to be put on the door to each floor, and made arrangements so that nobody could be coming in our hallway knocking on our door if we didn't want them there. They would have to come to that main door," he explained, "and call who they want, you know, before we would open the door to anyone."

It was kind of eerie standing there in the dim hallway while the rain kept up a continuous drizzle on the stoop. But the tenants warmed to their conversation, telling me of the filth, the overcrowding, and the lack of help or friends or just plain companionship. I asked why they never called the building or health departments to complain.

"None of us really know too much about that," said one woman.

"We wouldn't know who to call," chimed in another, an old woman with a gruff voice. "Everybody here's got a little sense," she said, "but they're not hip to the different laws and all that."

"Most everybody here is on welfare," explained the large person I'd talked to first. "So you know how that goes—the landlord does like he wants to do. He don't bother to fix up anything since welfare pays for all the expense, you know."

"He knows that most of the people ain't going to put up really a squawk." This from one of the fourteen-year-olds.

"How big is your room, approximately?" I asked a young man next to me.

"No bigger than a jail cell," he said. "That's what it is, I've been to jail so I know what it is, it's no bigger than a jail cell."

A kid of nineteen or twenty challenged him. "Oh man, what you mean a jail cell? You ain't never been to jail if you can say that."

"I think Brooklyn cells are a little bigger than what they have in Manhattan," added my first friend, quickly. And the crowd broke into small groups arguing spiritedly over the dimensions of a jail cell. On this note I took leave, and they waved me down the street, warning me to be careful.

"It ain't the junkies, it's the winos, sister," they yelled. "Watch out for those winos. They just as soon kill you as . . ." Their voices faded as I walked quickly into the wind and rain, exhilarated at having gotten one of the best spontaneous pieces of tape I'd ever get. In fact I was feeling so good that I walked all the way home, striding boldly through the rain, clutching my tape recorder under my raincoat, next to my spleen.

Over the door of the newsroom, where I work there hangs a sign: HOW MANY SIDES OF THE STORY DID YOU GET? Well, none of the SRO landlords would talk to me about conditions on their premises, so I did the next best thing, which works like this: You lie in wait for a public official who might have some answers you need, until he holds a press conference on any subject, and then you go and ask all sorts of questions about what you really want to know. I had to wait less than a week before the welfare commissioner and the head of the New York City Housing Authority held a joint news conference to announce the opening of a new shelter for families.

"There are presently only thirty-eight families on welfare still living in hotels," the commissioner announced triumphantly. This sounded peculiar to me, because the previous month I had been to the Concourse Plaza in the Bronx and had seen several hundred such families on public assistance being shuttled around by hotel authorities and specially hired guards. The key words were "living" and "family." The Bronx families weren't living per se, they were just there on temporary status, having been evicted, burned out, and the like. In some cases, however, they'd been "temporarily residing" in that hotel for more than a year.

The other word I was interested in was "family" because I also knew that thousands of welfare recipients who are single have no place to go other than these SRO hotels. At the time there were twenty-four thousand people in SRO houses, another seventy-three thousand in rooming houses, and a revolving population of six thousand or so in the lodging houses, with no figures available on SRO hotels. I asked the commissioner about this.

"I don't have a complete count on the number of single people in hotels and single room occupancies," he explained glibly, "but we have sent many thousands of such people on public assistance to these places."

"What's the maximum rent that you pay for a single hotel room?" I asked.

"Sorry, I can't tell you off the top of my head," he smiled.

"Is there a limit?" I persisted.

"There is a limit," he said, "for a single person, of five dollars a day per person set by the State. We often exceed that in family cases because it is not possible to obtain decent accommodations for five dollars a day per person."

"That's only for the room?" I was incredulous.

"That's right, the restaurant allowance is on top of that." I did some rapid mental arithmetic—for a family of four, five dollars per day per person amounts to six hundred dollars a month just in rent payments. If the City will pay this kind of money to landlords, I thought, no wonder tenants not on welfare are being forced out of SRO houses and hotels.

In Europe most of the major cities have boarding houses, hotels, and residences for single tenants. Living alone is an accepted way of life, and low-cost, clean accommodations are readily available. So I asked the chairman of the Housing Authority why little of this type of housing is built in New York City.

"We achieved an all-time record of housing starts in New York City last year," he said. "The Housing Authority achieved an all-time record of ten thousand units of public housing starts."

"Yes, but isn't that only for those over sixty-two years of age?" I queried. He looked uncomfortable.

"It's for families and for elderly individuals and families," he said. "But we operate with legal guidelines and constraints, and we don't have the ability to rent to young people who happen to be single. Of course, I'd like to see decent housing for everyone in need of it in our city."

"In other words, it pays to be married?" I had to bait him just a little.

"What? Oh, ha . . . ha," he chuckled nervously. "Well, I think it is a matter of social policy, ha, ha, that we still encourage marriage don't we?" He chuckled all the way out the door, and the news conference was over. But the issue wasn't closed for me.

Although reporters don't necessarily look for solutions to problems, I didn't feel I could do what had by this time turned out to be a long news series, just by laying out the facts about the appalling absence of intelligent approaches to the problem on the part of landlords, tenants, and city administrators. So I went to see Edna Baer, director of special purpose housing in the Housing Authority. In almost every city department there is a really capable woman who has been there for twenty years or so and knows all there is to know. Edna Baer is this kind of person, and I laid the problem in her lap. What to do about housing for single people? She felt that what she called congregate housing is the only answer.

"In lay terms," said Ms. Baer, "these are individual units, not necessarily with their own private baths, but with enough baths on the floor for the residents, and with community kitchens on each floor, where people could cook their meals. If you build without kitchens and private baths, your building can come in at a much lower cost and consequently a much reduced rental." She suggested built-in social service and medical programs, halfway houses with furnished rooms, full or partial board, linen allowances, and recreational programs for those residents with severe physical and mental health problems.

"What's needed is a serious program of designing, rehabilitating, and building adult residences and communal living projects," she explained. "SRO owners could be given guaranteed loans and tax exemption for rehabilitation of existing houses, for example."

"Why hasn't this been done?" I asked.

"We were successful in getting the federal government to make it possible to use federal funds for congregate housing, through the Housing Authority," she said. "But the Housing Authority has never implemented this kind of program, although we have urged them to do so. At the present time they have very limited funds for new construction, but they do have funds for leasing apart-

ments, and it would be a splendid idea if they would release some of these funds for this type of program."

"Of course," she added, "under federal guidelines, elderly people are given priority, and single people under
sixty-two must be defined as disabled under the Social
Security Act."

Having priority means little, as there is still no com-
prehensive government program to house the aged. Aside
from the periodic "cleanups" no real progress has been
made, either, for those under sixty-two. The single room
occupants continue to be the man on the totem pole
in housing priorities; they are still living in rooms no
larger than a prison cell. And forty years seems a long
time for Maria on East Twenty-first Street to wait.

No Alarm Will Ring

It must truly be a wonderful thing to wake up each morning knowing that the day belongs to you, that no alarm will ring and no one will tell you what to do or when to do it. Or that's what I thought as I lay in bed the morning after my editor had called me in and given me my choice of what to do for a series of special Christmas reports. I decided to go out and talk to some of the old people around town who enjoy this kind of freedom. Many of them, I found, are busy fighting to keep their freedom, to stay off welfare and take care of themselves. But with rents going up every year and housing in increasingly short supply, living on a fixed income has become more and more difficult.

Stella Allen, with whom I had worked on a voter registration drive for the elderly, heads the New York City

West Side Office for the Aging. I paid her a visit, and over a cup of tea in her office we discussed some of the acute problems that people over sixty have to face. There are more than fifty thousand older people living in public housing, Stella told me, but less than half live in buildings that were built to house the aged. Among this group, sixty percent are white, thirty percent black, and ten percent Puerto Rican; a direct inversion of the public housing pattern of younger people. Most white families have moved out to the suburbs, leaving their older relatives behind to live on three thousand dollars or less a year. Many give up food just to pay the rent.

"What will happen when these people are pushed off the Medicaid rolls?" asked Stella Allen. "Who's going to pay for glasses and dental care when they drop the eligibility ceiling for Medicaid? It's like signing their death warrant." When I left her she was shaking her head as she shuffled papers around on her desk. "It's totally irrational," she said. "They can't afford home services, and so they die alone in bed and lie there sometimes for weeks."

Many older people, as I found out on a visit to the Church of St. Paul and St. Andrew on West End Avenue, are winning the struggle for survival. St. Paul and St. Andrew is running an extensive program of free lunches for the elderly. I arrived there around 11:30 AM, and was warmly welcomed by the director of the program who introduced me around the room and gave me lunch. During the meal I talked with some of the old people at the same table. One ninety-six-year-old man named Mr. Rabinovitch told me that his wife had died, but that he still had many children and grandchildren.

"I live alone," he said in a thick Russian accent, "and

neighbors drop by every so often to see how I'm getting along." He explained that he had never had so much free time or such a good feeling about himself.

A woman of about the same age echoed his sentiments. "I read and clean my home although I can't move so quick," she said, in a quivering voice. "I used to work in a hospital, you know, like a nurse, but I'm ninety years old, and it's time to rest."

One old black woman in the lunch program disagreed; she was far from tired. "I love them, love them all," she cried. As soon as she had spotted my microphone she settled down, almost pushing me off the bench, to tell me the story of her checkered life as a dancer with jealous Latin lovers. She still had enough energy for loving. "I especially love the rabbis and the ministers," she cackled. "They tell me more about life than I already know, and I'm just startin' off to learn."

I asked another old woman why she had left Russia twenty-one years ago. "I was looking for . . . ," here she turned to a neighbor for a translation, "liberty, freedom. Here you dress you up, eat what you want, and nobody's staying in the night knocking on your door." She smiled happily.

While we were eating I had noticed a number of paintings on the walls of the room, and after lunch I was introduced to the artist. His name was Richard, and he was seventy-eight years old. He immediately took me in hand, chattering cheerfully about his life and former work as a copywriter, art director, and public relations man.

"All my life I've had to work to a deadline, for a salary, with executives having the power of life and death over me," he explained. "Once I was freed of that I was really able to branch out, let my own creativities blossom out."

Now, he told me, he had applied for a foundation grant to write poetry and take photographs. I was curious about other elderly people who had really found a new life after sixty-five, and Richard steered me toward Harold and Bea, aged sixty-nine and seventy-one, respectively, who were engaged to be married. They had met in the lunch program, and Harold asked Bea to marry him on the second date.

"I like her, I love her, I could see a picture of her in my future," he told me, grinning widely. Bea was hanging on to his arm for dear life. "When he asked me to become his wife after only taking me out twice, I said 'Dear, this is serious. Let's get engaged.' So the very next day he went out and bought me this lovely ring. We're the only older couple I know who has been engaged for so long—close to a year," she told me proudly.

Richard came back for me, and on an impulse I asked him if he had one wish, what it would be.

"To be twenty years younger," he answered promptly.

"Why?" I asked.

"Well," he replied, "I'm still capable of loving women. They fascinate me more and more as I get older. I see more of them now. When I was younger, all I saw was the outer shell, beautiful eyes and forms; now I see a great deal more. If I was twenty years younger I would also have more energy to devote to my work. I tire easily," he lamented, "and have to sleep a lot. But I'm my own boss. When I feel I have the time, I knock off and go to the theater. It's a wonderful thing to be freed of the need for money. I live on my social security and take all my meals here." He lowered his voice conspiratorially. "I don't know if you've noticed, but the chef is generous. Most times I don't even need to have dinner. Today we had an especially generous portion of chicken." He patted his pockets meaningfully, then waved goodbye.

Most of the old people in the city, unlike Richard and Harold and Bea, don't participate in such programs. Although many still live with their families, there are thousands who have no real home, no place to go when the weather is bad. You see them huddled in doorways, urinating on subway steps, and sleeping on closed newstands in underground alleyways.

As I left the Church of St. Paul and St. Andrew I decided to go to Central Park and talk to some of the senior citizens who inhabit the park benches. At Fifth Avenue and Seventy-second Street I spotted an interesting looking character sitting by himself, wearing a topcoat, hat, and dark woolen gloves, and holding a walking stick. Since we were the only two people in sight on that snowy day, I approached rather timidly and introduced myself.

His name was Robert Payne, and he was a partially disabled veteran. "I get one hundred and twenty-one dollars a month in veterans' benefits," he told me. "I feel just fine. It's a wonderful thing just to be alive." He stretched his arms high in the air. "You know, I see so many of these old guys creepin' around miserable. They're hurting, you know. Rich people sit around here. Never met a rich man yet who wasn't a stingy old miser. Me, I'm content just to breathe." He removed his hat and took a deep breath.

We chatted until it grew late and the air was colder, and I thought it was time to go. In parting, I asked Mr. Payne what plans he had for Christmas.

"Just trying to survive," he wheezed. "Another old man, eighty-six years old, has invited me to Schrafft's, and I know I'll get a good meal there."

"Robert Payne was only sixty-three." That's how I began my story on him when it went on the air. "I say only, because he has to wait two years for Social Security and he's not even sure he'll get it then because he has had a bullet in his spine since Normandy and hasn't been able to work much since." The station got one of the biggest responses it had ever had to this series, which ran during Christmas week. But half of Mr. Payne's story never got told and it was impossible to project on the air the dignity of this old man on the park bench, "just trying to survive."

Eventually I always got around to asking the old people what their plans were for the future, a question believe me, that took a lot of nerve. They'd look at me as if they couldn't believe that I'd asked, and I realized that not having an alarm ring in the mornings also means in many cases relinquishing the concept of a personal future. Some grinned and told me that they had big hopes; others were just waiting patiently; but all were damned glad to be alive.

After I left Robert I turned the corner and approached another elderly person, a woman this time. She wore a brown wool cap with tufts of white hair sticking up from under it. Her clothing was neat, and she was eating quietly from a grubby brown paper bag. When I approached the bench where she sat and asked if I might talk with her, she took a moment to smile at me and then furtively stuffed her ketchup sandwich back into the paper bag and started to rise slightly.

Looking directly into my eyes, still smiling, she whispered softly, "I know you," and started the most horrible, howling, animal-like sound that I have ever heard or hope to hear again from anything calling itself human.

For Whom the Bell Tolls

You may have remarked that it isn't only housing for the poor that often resembles prison cells. As you travel north from Manhattan, the Hutchinson River Parkway intersects with the New England Thruway just short of the city line. Shortly after the intersection, on your right, several groups of cement superstructures pop up, embedded in what appears from the highway to be swampland. When the gigantic development called Co-op City went up, drivers passing by would shake their heads at the strange sight of these fifty-story towers rising out of the marshes, miles from the nearest store, public transportation, or any form of life. Some three years after Co-op City was built, I decided to take a closer look—to get off the highway, wander around, and talk to some of the residents of the now occupied monstrosity.

Virtually a city in itself, Co-op City is the largest housing development in the world. Where else could you find a
credit union, an arts council, an ambulance corps, a
Sephardic synagogue, a young marrieds' club, a community ballet, community chorus, and a hot line all in the
same place? On my first visit early one evening, the Co-op
City tenants were having a huge "consumer fair" on the
top floor of a two-story recreation building. Balloons flew,
records played, and gaily-colored signs saying *Health,
Day Care, Education, Blood,* adorned the dozens of
booths spread over the L-shaped halls and on into the
large auditorium. There I found Don Phillips, the Co-op
City education chairman, who described the idea behind
this urban outpost.

"It's an attempt to put people back into control of their
own housing in the city," he said. "When the development
first opened, a multitude of families rushed to buy apartments. Some came from areas which were getting overcrowded, where the crime rate was on the rise; others were
simply pioneers excited by the challenge of a new kind of
life." And then, he explained, there were the financial ad-
vantages—for an initial purchase price of two thousand
dollars, a two-bedroom apartment would cost only one
hundred forty to one hundred fifty dollars in monthly
maintenance.

Phillips' feelings about Co-op City were echoed by
some of the other tenants he introduced me to.

"I was brought up in Brooklyn, and this represented a
new way of life, a clean slate, something we all could believe in," said one man.

"I thought it was a unique chance for the city to be
saved," said a woman. "We have relatively low-cost housing, plus a chance to control our own lives in the com-

munity. We elect the people to our board of directors that make decisions about the way things will be done in our community."

"You find that even with sixty thousand people you still have a community here?" I asked.

"Right, right. It's such a friendly atmosphere—everybody seems to be so pleasant. It's just like one big family."

Every big family has to have some children, I thought, and so I asked Don Phillips how children get along in Co-op City. He explained that there are close to twenty thousand kids in the development, and that when it opened three women raised twenty-five thousand dollars to start a day camp. The program has since been expanded to handle more than a thousand children. There is also a low cost nursery school run by the tenants, and a group called Services for Youth, formed by college students, which sponsors after-school clubs, tutoring, movies, and discussion groups for the younger kids.

I found sixteen-year-old Jeff Olison, a stocky, towheaded youngster, doing his turn at one of the fair booths, and I asked why he had wanted his family to move to Co-op City.

"What I wanted actually was a place where I could have a big enough room," he said. "We came from Forest Hills where rents are high but space is limited. Here I have all the area I want to play. We moved into one of the first buildings, and we waited so long to get in here, it's like a dream come true. I'm only sorry I can't go to school here."

"Where *do* you go to school?" I asked. Jeff was joined by Daisy, a young black girl with hair pulled back in braids. They explained that they had to travel all the way across the Bronx to go to high school because the schools in Co-op City were being built from the lower grades up.

Eventually, they said, there would be an educational park with all grade levels represented—but that was still in the future. And by the time the high school was completed, Jeff and Daisy would be out of school.

Co-op City was too big to get the feel of in just one visit. I felt that the fair was perhaps an artificial exhibition, with everyone on his or her best behavior. I was curious about crime, drugs, jealousies, greed, and neighborliness —some of the components of a true community. So a week later I came back to Co-op City unannounced. Cruising through the huge complex, this time in daylight, I examined the physical layout.

Co-op City is divided into five identical sections. One large street, Co-op City Boulevard, runs through the entire complex. The buildings themselves are located on small circles or loops, branching off from the boulevard. Three twenty-six-story triple-core buildings are on the outer rim of one loop, and directly below these, I discovered several smaller streets with townhouses. These three-story, two-family houses in groups of eight have one duplex and one ground floor apartment each. Then in the center of the loop, there's a two-story circular shopping center with bakeries, tailors, cleaners, stationery stores, beauty parlors, and the like.

Each shopping center has a co-operative supermarket in which the tenants invested fifty dollars each, sharing in the market's profits at the end of each year. The idea behind this, and other programs like it, is for people who live in Co-op City to feel in control of the flow of goods and services and to have a share in the income these bring. Such sharing is, however, a complicated affair, and must be carefully worked out by committees and directors and organizations.

The smell of fresh bread, incongruous in the wide-open,

concrete spaces, drew me into a bakery where lines of women, boys, and girls of all sizes, shapes, and ages waited to buy bread, bagels, and pre-fabricated Happy Birthday cakes in ten-, twelve-, and sixteen-inch sizes. There were only a few blacks or Latins sprinkled throughout the crowd. Many of the older women seemed to know one another, but as I went from store to store I sensed a superficial quality in the greetings. The salesgirls were smiling but slightly glassy-eyed, and I had the peculiar notion that everyone was trying not to cry.

I drove around the endless circles and loops watching women unload groceries from cars, mothers pushing strollers, and visiting relatives trying to find the right towers. Toddlers played on climbing sculptures, tepees, and natural rock formations scattered throughout sand gardens made of the salt sand-fill on which Co-op City had originally been built. Seemingly normal activities appeared to be acted out on a gigantic stage, with each participant for the most part ignoring his surroundings as if they were no more than a painted backdrop. It all seemed a bit unreal until I remembered Don Phillips' explanation that everything had been planned so that the tenants could exist at eye-level and never have to notice the huge buildings towering overhead.

A six-story garage sits at the entrance to each of the loops, because life here is impossible without a car. A subway link is planned to reach Co-op City by 1990, but in the meantime an automobile, or a bus to the subway, or an express bus to Manhattan are the only ways in or out. I stopped my car to talk to a group of teen-agers who were horsing around in front of a community building, their exuberant high spirits in sharp contrast to the subdued "normality" of the rest of the population.

"How do you like it here?" I asked, introducing myself.

"We can't get around," shrugged one girl. "No place to go."

"We always have to walk," complained another youngster. "We've got bicycles, but if we use them we'll get a ticket, because we're only allowed to ride on the cycle path which is a tiny circle that goes no place. We can't ride from one section to another to visit friends, because that's a ten-dollar ticket."

"What about social life?" I asked.

"Well, we hang around the community center at night when it's cold," a boy explained. "But if we sit where we're sitting now, a cop comes down the stairs and says to get out."

"Yeah," chimed in another girl. "There are far too many security guards."

"When you need them they're not around," said another kid. "But when you don't need them and don't want to see them, they're around."

Although each building in Co-op City has floor captains, the development still employs a staff of thirty-five security guards who patrol with walkie-talkies and nightsticks. But while residents I talked to agreed that the guards are comforting to have around, and crime statistics here are generally lower, there had still been several purse snatchings, and only a few weeks earlier a woman was assaulted and raped upon entering her own apartment. Several other crimes had taken place, and the kids were right —the guards were nowhere to be found at the time.

The head of the tenants' association later told me that there were also serious complaints about the lack of other vital services such as hospitals, ambulances, a fire department, and post office. Although the pioneer spirit was much in evidence throughout Co-op City, the signs of stress were there as well, and some tenants found a vast difference between the dream and the reality. Originally, maintenance for Co-op City housing had been pegged at around twenty-five dollars a room per month. Now, sky-rocketing building costs have brought the maintenance charges closer to sixty dollars a room. The tenants I talked to said they would continue to fight for fixed interest rates and tax relief, but not too many were moving out. I asked one tenant why.

"Well," he sighed, "it's a new life, a better life for my family. I think it's probably a dream everyone has had at one time or another."

"Has your dream been realized?" I asked.

"I would say about eighty percent," he answered thoughtfully. "The other twenty percent, well, as in every co-operative you have problems. Primarily our problems existed with hastily constructed buildings. Then rent and maintenance increases, that will probably make a lot of people move. But frankly, I could say, more than any-thing else, there's a lot more good than bad."

When the New York City sanitation workers went out on strike and tenants had to carry garbage down twenty and thirty stories, there was a lot more bad than good, however. And one afternoon, a bankrupt businessman climbed onto his Co-op City window ledge and jumped from one of the towers. The news photos showed his neigh-bors leaning out of their windows in the surrounding build-ing core, avid eyewitnesses, but just a fraction too far away to reach for him.

The people who live in Co-op City still believe that giant buildings won't dehumanize people as long as a sense of community remains. I wasn't so sure. Was their "sense of community" an illusion? Co-op City, I told myself as I headed down the parkway is still, after all, in New York City, the only "community" in the world that could successfully absorb a mini-city within its boundaries without even a ripple. Anywhere else in the world, Co-op City would have a constant horde of visitors and curiosity seekers waiting to see the rise or fall of this sixty-thousand-person experiment. As it was, I was driving the only car on this stretch of the road, headed back toward my radio station at Fortieth and Park, and a funny idea kept nagging me. I was remembering Donne's admonition: "No man is an island. . . . Therefore send not to know for whom the bell tolls. . . ." Well, what if you live in a place where you have to ask that question day after day after day?

PART II

FEBRUARY 18, 1974, FLATLANDS, BROOKLYN, USA—*The two Brooklyn youngsters, both white, around fourteen and fifteen years old, didn't seem to know there was an energy crisis going on. They "borrowed" a car to go for a joy ride, and when the helicopter spotted them in a swampy section of Flatlands they had just changed drivers. One of them proudly swung the car back and forth across the muddy lane, while the other hollered in glee. The sound of the police chopper warned them that trouble was coming, so they opened the car door and, piling out on either side, began to run for it.*

The pilot wove back and forth, cutting off their routes of escape, forcing them back toward the car, and after landing, took them into custody and to the Sixty-ninth

Precinct, where they were booked for grand larceny of an auto as youthful offenders.

The police pilot had been out on a routine photo-taking mission, an intelligence chore he told me he performed every day.

"It took less than sixty seconds from the time I spotted the car until the computer in my copter told me it was a stolen vehicle," he boasted. "You can't outrun a chopper with a car," he told me proudly, "and you sure as hell can't do it on foot."

More than a Note from Mama

Over the past century civil liberties have been extensively analyzed and defined in the United States by both legislative bodies and by the Supreme Court. All citizens are considered to have an inalienable right to education, equal employment opportunity, to housing, to welfare, and to a habitable environment. All have the right to participate and protest; but these rights are largely denied to over forty percent of our population—the people between the ages of one and eighteen. In investigating the fledgling Children's Liberation Movement, I found that children don't even have the right to consent to the broadcast of their own voices. They are often treated as appendages or the property of their parents or a custodial agency.

Under New York law, minors may open a savings account but have trouble opening checking accounts. They may own real estate but not stocks, and adults are reluctant to do business with anyone under eighteen, because the word of a minor may not be contractually binding. In fact, as I found out talking to a ten-year-old friend of mine, kids ordinarily may not even legally be treated by a doctor or a psychiatrist without their parents' consent. "I was number one hundred and nineteen or something on the line at the clinic, and after waiting one hundred and eighteen people, the guy said you need your parents, even if you do have a note and a passport."

"Who was this guy?" I asked.

"He was some doctor in his eighties, an old man," replied my young friend. "He worked for the Department of Health."

"What were you asking him to do?" I wanted to know.

"I asked him for a smallpox shot for when I'm going to Europe. I gave him a note from my mother and my passport, and he rejected it." My friend was outraged—with some justification I thought—and I decided to look further into the matter. My first stop was the Citizens Committee for Children, located in a small, serious-looking East Side building. Despite the grimness of its offices, the Citizens Committee has an outstanding reputation as the only organization to do anything meaningful about the liberation of children. I spoke with Betty Bernstein, explaining that I was seeking information about the Children's Lib movement. "What Children's Lib movement?" she laughed. "Why, even for children to get inoculations in school," she told me, "parents must give informed consent. So every time the parent can't provide a service and the school or Health Department wants to provide it, you have to get consent for the specific thing." The Citizens Committee feels parents should have a role in their children's health where possible, but are concerned that under the present law, for example, an unmarried mother under eighteen could have the right to consent for the medical care of her child, but not for herself.

Ms. Bernstein sent me downstairs to see Leah Marks, a very serious dark-haired woman who is the attorney for the Citizens Committee. I asked what kind of psychological counseling is available to youngsters, and if they must have their parents' consent to be treated by a psychiatrist.

"There are guidance counselors in every school," she said, "but at the same time the guidance counselor is working for the school system. So that sometimes a child may say something the counselor feels the principal should know about despite the fact that the child came there for a confidential discussion. Also reports like this sometimes find their way into the suspension files years later. The guidance counselor's files and the guidance counselor's mouth are simply not shut to an extent that permits him to have a confidential trusting relationship with the child."

Minors lose out on other rights, too, I found. In New York State all minors generally have the right to stay in school until the age of twenty-one, yet many students are systematically pushed toward leaving school at the earliest possible age. Ms. Marks cited the famous Franklin K. Lane case where six or seven hundred students had received letters saying "You have not been coming to school regularly. You are seventeen and no longer on the rolls."

"Many of the students were told that they were truanting regularly and that there would be no place for them from now on, and yet they had in fact been attending school," she said. "One girl actually got this letter while working as a typist in the principal's office. She was actually in school, and the letter told her that she could no longer enter the building."

"What did she do?" I asked.

"She went home," said Ms. Marks, "thinking that her life had been ruined, and it was only when the case came to court that her right to return to school was vindicated."

Children are denied their rights to education in other ways. If you are a minor and live alone or with a friend's parents, you will not be enrolled in school, since you only enjoy your right to education with your parent's or legal guardian's consent. Most boards of education say that such permission must be forthcoming in writing before a child can be enrolled in city schools. Often, until recently, even when a child got into school, he found himself suspended without even knowing why. It was not rare for a child to come home with a note to the parent saying, "Your child is suspended, keep him home every day until 3:00 PM." It is now illegal to suspend a student for more than five days without a formal hearing.

As the chairman of the American Civil Liberties Union, Aryeh Neier, explained to me, it has been traditional to view the child within the school the same way people in other compulsory institutions are viewed—the prisoner in prison, the mental patient in the hospital, or the soldier in the armed forces.

"Schools see kids as people who have to be programmed through the system," he sighed, "for the benefit of the institution, rather than as a whole person entitled to the exercise of constitutional rights."

The courts are now ruling on cases challenging students' rights to dress, search and seizure, and free speech. But the United States Supreme Court has upheld plea bargaining, a common practice in our courts which can be disastrous for young people. The defendant is encouraged to "cop out," or plead guilty in return for a lesser charge; the only hitch is that the lesser charge is often not forthcoming. The child has pleaded guilty and has never gone to trial!

The Supreme Court has also ruled that under the United States Constitution minors do not have the right to a jury trial. They must, however, receive warnings of their right to counsel when arrested, as I found out when I went to see my old friend Tom Kelley, a lanky Irishman with a wide grin who is in charge of community relations at the Twenty-fourth Precinct.

"Tom, tell me what happens when a kid is arrested," I said.

"Well," he replied, unfolding his long-legged frame out of the hard chair he'd been sitting in, "we'll try and get the facts from the youngster at the scene. Sometimes they refuse to identify themselves, and we don't know how old they are, so we bring them here to my office and try to get in touch with the parents, the school, or the legal guardian. From then on we try to get the parents to take the child. A lot of parents won't do this—they say they have no control over the kid, and then it becomes another problem."

When this happens, Tom told me, the children are sent to a shelter until the case comes to court. The law divides children into two categories: juveniles, those under sixteen, and youthful offenders, those between the ages of sixteen and twenty-one. Aryeh Neier had told me that originally the designation "delinquent child" was meant to protect the youngster. Once a child was adjudged a juvenile delinquent, many states would allow this delinquency judgment to be sealed or kept confidential after a given period of time.

"Is it true that the judge doesn't have to state his reasons for judging a child a juvenile delinquent?" I asked Neier.

"A judge, of course, doesn't have to state the reasons for finding a person guilty of a crime either," Neier pointed out. "But a finding of guilty in a criminal case is more susceptible to review by higher courts than is a finding of juvenile delinquency for a child. If a youngster is found to be a 'person in need of supervision,' he or she may be taken from the home and sent to a Juvenile Center."

Over the years there has been, periodically, a lot of public outcry about these juvenile detention facilities, most of which are located far from the children's families and probation officers. Conditions are terribly overcrowded, and small boys are often locked into a small cubicle to sleep with older boys, a situation that encourages the rapes and other perversions so often reported. I wondered if this form of supervision didn't border on cruelty, and trekked over to the Society for the Prevention of Cruelty to Children to find out.

The SPCC is located in a huge East Side brownstone, a curious building with self-locking elevators, iron grates, and the like, which looks as though it should house the Society for the Prevention of Cruelty to Brownstones. I asked Mr. Thomas Becker, the director, for his definition of cruelty to children.

"Let's say a willful failure to provide the medical or psychiatric help that a child needs; a failure to provide him, if the means are available, with reasonably decent food, clothing, and shelter," he said. "Then we get into a much more nebulous area, emotional neglect, which is a form of cruelty, much more difficult to establish and identify, but possibly even more damaging to the child than an isolated case of physical abuse. The unfortunate thing is that the SPCC can only deal with parental cruelty and not the cruelty of society to children."

I understood what he was talking about, since I was becoming increasingly aware of the kind of cruelty the average young person must face in every aspect of life—from his search for work to the simple act of shopping for Christmas presents. I decided to take the issue to some children and hear what they had to say, and I went out to my street corner, which happens to be Ninety-eighth and Broadway, with my tape recorder.

"Some grown-ups think they're better than children, and they don't give no rights to children at all. I'm already eleven and I think I'm old enough to have a job now," said one little girl to my question about whether being young was a problem.

"They don't use delivery boys of ten years old," responded a friend of hers, angrily. "They use them sixteen or eighteen years old."

Even worse than the lack of employment opportunities was the strong discrimination these children met with from shopkeepers in the neighborhood, as well as in department stores downtown.

"I had a birthday present; it was a Heavy Chevvy," said a very bright looking eight-year-old to me. "But I already had one, so I tried to go and return it. And there are two people in the shop. There's this nice guy who will let you return things and who won't charge you tax, and there's this guy who charges you tax and won't let you return anything unless you're an adult." He seemed frustrated.

Some kids fight back, establishing spheres of influence for themselves in an adult world. Eighteen-year-old Devon Black, whom I've known since he was thirteen, became interested in broadcasting and set up a radio station in his living room. He called it WWAC, and he used to sit and practice for hours, being alternately a disc jockey, newscaster, program director, and chief engineer. When I went to talk to him about children and children's rights he was actively involved in local politics, but I managed to catch him between campaigns. I asked how he got started in politics.

"I started out doing leafletting, handing out buttons on street corners, and I did that for seven years; then I moved up quickly, or slowly, depending on your perspective, until I was campaign manager for an assembly candidate."

"Did you find any obstacles?" I asked.

"People in the political process tend to be a little edgy about listening to new voices," said Devon, "particularly when those voices are young. The whole thing about being anyone in the political system seems to be experience and age. I felt that while I had enough experience, my age was holding me back."

"What about your less aggressive friends?" I asked. "What will happen to them in later years because of the handicap of being young?"

"I'm not sure," he said. "I think a lot of people I know have been held back because of their age and this notion that you can't be anything unless you're older. Unfortunately, when they reach the age where they're allowed to make the decisions on who does what and when, they will, unless I'm really reading them wrong, also discriminate against the young."

Another eighteen-year-old acquaintance of mine, named Adam, had been composing music—good music—for more than a decade. "Would the adult structure permit a child to play an important role in society?" I asked.

"The first thing society has to do is get rid of the idea that a young person isn't capable of doing certain things," he said. "We had this idea with blacks that they couldn't do certain things because they were 'inferior'; and with women that 'their place was in the house.' As far as a child's being capable of making a contribution is concerned—well, I was, and I'm not unique."

But what about the unlucky ones, I wondered, the ones who have trouble making it on their own? A minor may receive welfare if he or she is over seventeen, living alone, and has been judged an emancipated minor. The welfare worker makes this decision based on such facts as whether or not the minor has a high school diploma, or perhaps whether he or she has previously supported himself or herself, or whether he or she has a child. Unfortunately, I found, it often happens that the only way a young runaway girl can get information about welfare is through a pimp. The streets are full of youngsters in limbo simply because the benefits of adult society have been denied to them and they have nowhere to turn for help. After I had finished the story on children's rights I wondered what kind of impact, if any, it would have. I knew I had learned something—in the past I had rarely asked for a child's opinion of anything, almost never interviewed a youngster on any subject, despite the fact that more than half of the city's population is under eighteen. Doing this story broadened my perspective. Last Veterans Day I interviewed two ninety-year-olds and a twelve-year-old about Watergate, patriotism, and the parade, and the answers and descriptions I got were better "sound" than I'd had all year. In doing an obituary on Adam Clayton Powell, some of the best impressions were those of an eight-year-old girl who'd overheard adults talk and had read about the congressman in the papers. I now go out of my way to talk to kids about the Middle East crisis, politics, corruption, and strikes, as well as Macy's Thanksgiving Day parades.

As it turned out, I wasn't the only one thinking about children's role in an adult society. This is one of hundreds of letters I received after the story on children's rights went on the air:

Barbara, where do you get your ridiculous idea that a child (you're talking about from seven years old) should be recognized as to their ability as an adult. I pay this boy $10.00 for

three and a half hrs and an expense lunch, two hamburgers, a
bowl of salad and a glass of milk, then half of a Sara Lee,
cherry filled cake, that piece he had was 6″ x 4″ in size with two
glasses of ice tea. I had an other youngster that shoveled five
feet of snow on the sidewalk just exactly six minutes — $5.00.
I wouldn't have him any more and the $10.00 boy will find
more work and longer hours or his future will be ruined. Your
funny I wonder who gave you this break. Children today tell
teachers, parents and all authoritative people what they will
do. Your harmful and should stop.

The Most Frightened People
I Have Ever Met

Edward, who is thirteen years old, lives on the West Side of Manhattan and attends a private school. Almost every-day on the way home from school he is ripped off. He will remove his tie and watch, and rumple his jacket to avoid being noticed as he walks the block from Broadway to West End Avenue. But the older kids get him just the same. One day as he went to the delicatessen a block from school to get lunch for a teacher, a gang of older boys threw him down and stole his bus pass, watch, and wallet.

Edward's case is not unusual—something like this goes on every day somewhere in the city, and has for a number of years, as I found out when I talked with a group of black ten-year-olds in Queens. They would only meet me at a "safe house," the home of a white friend who attended parochial school. They came in one by one to avoid attracting attention. One kid, whom we'll call Steve, told me that he had been robbed repeatedly in the Jamaica ghetto he used to live in.

"I was about eight years old, and the guys used to take me every day, so my mother had to go up to school, and the principal called the other boys' parents, and they all had to talk about it. But nothing happened. So my mother moved here and put me in a better school so I wouldn't get beat up any more."

"Did that make things any better?" I asked.

"No. I was ripped off again, last week. A bunch of kids pulled me over to the curb and told me to give them my money."

"Did they have a knife or anything?" I probed.

"No," said Steve. "One of them just hit me in the chest, and you see, I didn't have any money, so they beat me up after that."

"How old are you?" I asked him, almost as an afterthought.

"Twelve."

Almost all of the children seemed to think it was better not to resist. One of them, Robert, who was smaller than the others, with very dark skin and a wiry body, was adamant on the subject.

"If I have any money and they ask me for it, I say 'man I ain't got no money,' like that. If they hit me, I let them hit me. I got my money tooken away a coupla times. I think the best thing to do, if you got two boys gettin' ready to take your money, is to just give it to them, and then discuss it with your mother or somebody like that."

After a series of consultations with his mother, Edward —the boy whose story had originally aroused my interest in crimes against children—agreed to come to my home for a taped interview. "There are two types of muggers," he reported. "There's the type that will ask you for, let's say, a dime, and if you won't give it to him he'll leave you alone." He gave a long sigh.

"Then there's the type of muggers that will approach you and ask for a dime, quarter, or what have you, and if you don't give it to them, they will threaten you with violence." Here Edward's voice broke, but he went on. "You know, there's no other choice to take. You have to give them whatever you have."

"How can you tell which type of mugger is approaching you?" I asked.

"You can't tell, really," he said. "But it goes by groups. It depends upon the size of the group."

I asked Edward whether or not he felt the police would protect him. "They consider me a kid. If a kid asks for help or screams for help or whatever, which would be the natural thing to do," he said, "they wouldn't listen to him at all. They'd just think he's playing around with other kids and looking for attention, you know, just having fun."

I was shocked by the terror I found in these young people. Many of them had no one to turn to and were afraid, not only for themselves but for their parents. Especially afraid are the ones who live alone with their mothers. There have been cases in Brooklyn and the Bronx where gangs have set fire to a house, killing several families, out of vindictiveness when a child or his parents have refused to cooperate in one way or another. Lionel, a junior high school student, told me that he had received a threatening phone call from the older brother of one of his school friends.

"His big brother asked me for fifty cents when he got on the phone," said Lionel. "So I started out giving them money and everything. First I gave them four dollars, and then he asked me to snatch a pocketbook or get some money from my mother. He'd say he wanted lipstick, makeup, or identification as well. And then he wanted to know did my mother go to work 'cause he'd try to make me get it from my mother."

After talking with the children in the safe house in Queens, I phoned for an appointment with the principal of their school, saying only that it was a matter of urgency. When I got to the school a number of clerks, secretaries, and teachers in the office tried to handle the matter, but I would not state my business and asked them to call the principal. He was shocked by what I told him—a list of dates and locations of robberies and names of the seventh and eighth graders doing the extorting. True to my promise, I never mentioned the names of the victims. Unlike many other principals, this one accepted full responsibility for his pupils while they were traveling to and from school, but he seemed to feel the only thing he could do to help would be to encourage students not to carry money, saying, "If kids have to buy a gym uniform or something, we encourage parents to write out a check."

A few weeks earlier I had interviewed a Bronx principal about reading scores; now I called him back to ask about the rate of violence and extortion at his school.

"Often when I leave school," he said "there are several kids from the high school waiting for younger girls, and they each have four or six heavy chains slung around their necks. That's enough to frighten anyone. In this general area there have been cases of adults extorting money from children at the bus terminal."

"What have you done about this situation?" I asked.

"Well the police sent in undercover operatives," he

sighed. "They're limited in their manpower, but they usually have at least one full-time person on what they call school relations, meaning these kinds of activities."

I visited a number of high schools, including the High School of Music and Art, a school for gifted children from all over the city. The school's administrators admitted to having had a rash of muggings in the hallways for a week or so, but proudly told me that the youngsters involved had been caught promptly. However, when we got onto the subject of what happens to their students on the way home from school, around the corner, across the street, in the park, and on subways and buses, the story was different.

"We simply cannot assume responsibility for the kids outside of school," an assistant principal told me frankly. "We know they are mugged and harassed." Someone had to be assuming this responsibility, I thought. Someone had to be trying to protect these kids. But who? To find out I called on my old friend Eldridge Waithe, who used to be a police chief and was then chief of security for the Board of Education.

"Our department gets three or four complaints a week. They're students asking for twenty-five, ten, five cents," he told me. "They say 'gimme a quarter or I'll punch you in the mouth,' things like that. A lot of students take intimidation, robbery, extortion, without reporting it—they're afraid of it, but they just see it as part of the scene. If we could establish a pattern of some sort of identification, we'd be able to cut down on the number of extortions that take place. We try to protect kids going to and from the school, but we can extend ourselves only so far."

I found that police are rarely called in, by child, school, or parent. In one investigation I began, it turned out that the kid extorting the money was himself the victim of older, teen-age extortionists, to whom he had to give so much money each week that he had to turn to mugging to meet the payments. As I talked with youngsters from all over the city, and found a pattern of daily extortion, threats, and unbelievable fear, what shocked me most was that I wasn't surprised. Parents, poor and rich alike, live with the fact that kids grow up in an atmosphere of fear—fear of failure, fear of street gangs. The constant fear of being uprooted must seem gigantic to a child. Alvin Toffler tells of a twelve-year-old girl who was sent to a supermarket three blocks away from her home. She returned in fifteen minutes and reported that it wasn't there; it must have been torn down. She had unwittingly taken a wrong turn, come upon a hole in the ground, and cheerfully gone home—after all, buildings had been going up and coming down around her all her life.

Fifteen Thousand
Three Hundred and
Forty-Three Children

One of the most difficult assignments I ever had began innocuously enough when the assistant news director called me in to investigate rumors of trouble on Manhattan's Lower East Side, where two patrolmen had just been shot. I still remember the skimpy fact sheet he gave me. The two cops, one black, one white, were partners who had been shot in the back by one or more unknown assailants. I was to fill in the general background of violence, find out how far it was likely to go, and tell the world about it in my investigative report. Maybe eight two-minute segments, all neatly wrapped up for the air.

The first thing I remember doing is going to a map to establish my perimeters, trying to determine what exactly comprised the Lower East Side, one of the least familiar sections of a city I knew well.

I finally decided that the Lower East Side area runs roughly south from Fourteenth Street to Water Street between Third Avenue and the East River. Long a haven for immigrants, the area had over the past quarter of a century seen Puerto Ricans, blacks, and Chinese begin to replace the young Jewish families who in turn were moving to the Bronx, Brooklyn, and the West Side of Manhattan. But in the early seventies, the melting pot had turned into a pressure cooker, and I had to capture its explosion in an eight-part series.

Rather than go to political leaders or the police first, I decided to hang out at a couple of community meetings, the most interesting of which was likely to be the district school board meeting. It was apparent that the focal point of most of the tension in the community, which had been going on for five or six years, was the school system. In fact, before the city school system was decentralized in 1970, the then-current district school board had dissolved itself, claiming that disputes within the community made it impossible to administer the school district.

Under the 1970 decentralization law, a new nine-member board was elected by parents and other community residents of what became District One. But by the time I came on the scene, three of these board members had already resigned, claiming physical threats and harassment. One vacancy was filled, leaving a total of seven board members. These seven stood divided along racial lines on virtually every issue, four blacks and Puerto Ricans to three whites, making it impossible to get the five votes required for a final decision on any subject.

At a community meeting of a loose-knit group called the Education Coalition, Lucy Toomey, a paraprofessional in the schools, filled me in on the situation.

"It's the times," she said. "They try, everyone tries, but it seems like there's a lot of ignorance. The adults fail as well as the kids. The kids go to the school; the kids fail; the parents are disgraced; the school blames them; and the parents blame the school. We're supposed to fix the situation with good will, and we can't," she complained.

Members of the school board in District One wouldn't agree to sit down together for a round table discussion on tape, so I went to their homes and offices individually. Nettie DiMauro lived in a neatly kept brownstone walkup.

"We can never agree," she began tentatively. "Each side feels they're right. . . . When I make up my mind this is the way I wanta vote, this is the way I wanta vote, period. And I don't compromise very easily; I don't like to be blackmailed into compromising. So I guess the more they push, the more I stand my ground." There seemed to be nothing further to say on that subject, so I went in search of another board member, Henry Ramos, whom I found also in a walkup, the home of a local poverty agency. His small office was overflowing with people, and it wasn't easy to talk at any length. I asked Ramos if, unlike Nettie DiMauro, he felt any compromise could be worked out at this point.

"Well," said Ramos, "the human pain that the non-white members of the board have endured the last year and a half will take a long, long time to heal."

"What kind of human pain, Mr. Ramos?" I asked.

"Oh, the arbitrary decisions," he replied. "Depriving the non-white members of the board of due process, denying them the information that they need in order to be able to function as board members, denying them the right to be in on policy-making decisions."

Evidently the school board was an important medium of

political and social expression—yet I found that in the eyes of some people involved the issues were very different.

"I think," one of the parents said to me, "I think that the local school board should understand we're here for a purpose of children, nothing else. And if they cannot see it with us, then they should not have decentralization. I was once very much for decentralization, but I cannot say that I am now. I feel that it created a power struggle, and I feel that it is a hazard."

I found out how much of a hazard a few days later, at a school board meeting. Arriving late, I was drawn to a crowd of people standing around wearing skullcaps and getting ready for what looked like a protest or a demonstration. But as I neared the group, suddenly it uncoiled like a snake, with people running off in different directions into the night. I started to follow. Glass started smashing everywhere, and at first I thought it had come from the projects overhead. But then I saw a squat older man, also wearing a skullcap and carrying a stout stick, fling a bottle of what looked like club soda to the ground. Glass went flying again and when I looked down a small piece of my leg also lay on the sidewalk. I too ran then, away from the group, realizing that I had just made the acquaintance of one of the toughest commando groups I had seen since the war in Europe. Their speed and coordination were perfect. Police came and they ran off, weaving down the streets between the buildings.

Blood trickling down my leg, I went back to the school to get the story. But I was never to get inside—not that night, anyway. At the school door I ran into my old friend Irving Newman, otherwise known as the Herring King because he imports herring from Reykjavik. He was holding his head with grief. We made our way to my car, and Newman told me what had happened.

"I was approximately five minutes late in coming to the meeting," the big man told me as we sat in the car. "I saw three or four police cars outside and I says 'Well, there's gonna be a lot of commotion today.' As I was walking in the door of the school, a huge fella was unfurling an Israeli flag and I thought, 'It'll be a warm night tonight.' " As far as I could tell from what Newman was saying, a group of people claiming to be members of the Jewish Defense League had simply taken over the meeting. I was amazed, but Newman was near tears.

"For the first time in my life," he said, "I was ashamed to call myself a Jew. When I saw what the JDL did at that meeting . . ." I didn't know what to say, and for a while the two of us sat in silence, staring through the windshield of my car at the darkened street.

The police cars, men, and horses waiting outside were to become a familiar part of the pattern. The white members of the school board began to get anonymous telephone calls from people claiming to be Black Panthers, who would threaten their lives if they came to the meetings. The black and Puerto Rican board members got similar calls purporting to be from the JDL. I began to wonder if this sort of thing went on in other school districts, or if the violence was confined to District One, and I started attending a few board meetings in other districts. At one meeting in East Harlem, the proceedings opened with the board chairman screaming "Motherfucker!" into the open microphone as she banged the gavel wildly on the table and ended when the district superintendent, apparently in a state of shock, was removed by police, who had been waiting in the wings. There were more children than adults in the audience, and as I left the school I noticed more children outside attracted no doubt by the sirens and police cars.

"What happened?" I asked them, pretending ignorance.

"Well, oh man," stammered one youngster excitedly, "I heard, I mean, someone shot a man."

"Yeah," echoed the others, nodding wisely. They hung about for a little longer and then drifted back home for dinner.

Meanwhile, on the Lower East Side, the climate of violence continued, and it was revealed that District One children consistently had the lowest reading scores in the city. I called the district superintendent, Carl Erdberg, for an interview, and I asked why his schoolchildren couldn't read.

"Many of the children in this district speak Spanish and never take the reading test in English," said Erdberg. "We are one of the most, if not the most, language-retarded districts in the city, because seventy percent of our children are of Spanish-speaking background. The hurdles we must surmount involve not only teaching the fundamentals but the bilingual problem." Erdberg felt there was hope in a federally-funded program called More Effective Schools, or MES, which is supposed to provide for smaller classes and a larger teaching staff, in selected schools within a particular district. Unfortunately, opinion within District One is not unanimously in favor of the program.

"It discriminates against the children in the non-MES schools," explained Henry Ramos. "Last year we had three and a half million dollars of extra funds for extracurricular programs to help those who are having problems. If you give one and a half million to two schools and then take the other million and a half and try to distribute it among the other seventeen schools, I don't think that's fair."

"Another thing that bothers me very much," he continued, "is that PS 188, which has almost a million dollars in MES funds to pay the salaries of between twenty-five and forty extra teachers, has not hired one black or Puerto Rican to teach in that school. That really bothers me. For some reason or other, in that school, they have been discriminating against the hiring of blacks or Puerto Ricans."

Board member Nettie DiMauro, saw things differently. "Before I voted on that program," she said, "I paid a visit to one of the schools without anyone knowing I was going there. And what I saw convinced me that it's a very good program for the children. The atmosphere in the school was conducive to learning. There were no children running around; when we walked into a classroom, the children just looked up for one second and went right back to their work. Every child was occupied; you didn't hear any teachers yelling and screaming at the children."

I asked Lisle Brown, a third board member, if he thought the MES program was beneficial to the kids. "It doesn't really offer anything new," he said. "It acts primarily as an employment bureau for unemployed professionals." No one, after three years, was able to say conclusively whether or not the children were learning more in MES schools.

What kind of children were they, I wondered, these kids with the lowest reading scores in the city? Of some eighteen thousand students in District One, seventy percent are Puerto Rican or of other Spanish-speaking origin, fifteen percent black, five percent Chinese, and the remaining ten percent are of Polish, Italian, and Jewish descent. The ethnic conflict was largely between parents of school-children and other residents of the community, of whom only fifty percent were minority group members. The local Democratic district leader, an old friend, pointed out that the Grand Street project, a co-operative development whose population is ninety-nine percent middle class and Jewish, has eighty-three percent of its eligible residents registered to vote; they usually produce an eighty percent turnout at the polls, wielding control over school board elections, among others.

There were many groups engaged in political struggles on the Lower East Side, but perhaps the strongest point of conflict was around the teachers' union, the United Federation of Teachers. Charges and countercharges flew back and forth; principals were accused of using school personnel to solicit votes for union candidates; the teachers accused the parents' slate of wanting to do away with due process and with hiring unlicensed teachers. There was bitterness at the lack of Spanish-speaking teachers on the one hand; on the other, ethnic hiring of teachers was denounced.

Mark Pessen, a young teacher who lives on the Lower East Side told me, "People have to be taught that the real problems in the school system are not those of race. The racial issue is used by people in power to prevent any education from going on." Pessen and I talked about educators who insist on blaming school problems on the fact that the school is not homogeneous, and Pessen charged the teachers' union president, Albert Shanker, with using racism for his own ends. I had interviewed Shanker at length during the hearings held by the National Commission on Civil Rights, asking him then if he thought Puerto Rican kids were getting a good education.

"I think the school system does not do a good enough job for them, but I do not think it does a good enough job for any of the children," he had said, ducking the issue.

It certainly wasn't doing a good job for the children of

District One, where a new superintendent, Luis Fuentes, was hired to replace retiring Superintendent Carl Erdberg. Fuentes was charged with anti-Semitism when he criticized a group of parents. "Not so," he said. "I cursed them all equally, blacks, Jews, and Puerto Ricans." Fuentes put arroz con pollo on the lunchroom menu and sent the menu to the children's homes, with a slate of board candidates printed on the other side, for every parent to read. Nonetheless, when new elections were held in May 1973, the slate supporting Fuentes was defeated, and whites retained majority control of the new board. The Justice Department was called in to investigate charges of racial discrimination during the elections. A lawsuit was brought, charging that Spanish-speaking parents had been prevented from voting. Instances were cited in which middle-class white districts turned out thousands of votes and Spanish residents were turned away on technicalities. A new election was held and the board remained split. The Supreme Court has said that if one district is found to discriminate, then the whole system may be presumed to be segregated. In Boston, federal funds had been taken away on these grounds, and the federal funds in District One seemed similarly threatened.

In the fall of 1973 my radio station got a call that hundreds of mounted police and police cars had surrounded a school. I was sent out to investigate, and found that it was simply another District One school board meeting in progress. Police were asking for identification before letting the public into the school auditorium; a troop of mounted police stood ready in the schoolyard; and up on stage one half of the school board was actively leading the five to six hundred people in yelling and hooting down the other board members, so that no meeting could take place.

The board later retired backstage and ousted Superintendent Fuentes; the next day a court order put him back in. And so it went until a higher court finally removed him from District One.

Board meetings came to resemble riot scenes. The issue had grown so out of proportion, that I concluded the only way to keep the kids learning on the Lower East Side would be to declare it a protectorate and have some outside educational body come in to administer the district.

Ironically enough, the reason for which I had originally been sent down to the Lower East Side, the killing of two cops, turned out to have been drug-related and had little, if anything, to do with racial tensions or community board politics. Shortly after I learned this from street sources, the police commissioner confirmed it; how drugs came into the matter was never made clear. But dead is forever, and forever are the fifteen thousand three hundred and forty-three children in District One who never really learned to read.

PART III

There is a woman who, announcing herself alternately as Sarah Vaughn or Mrs. Johnson (a pseudonym), tracks down reporters or other personnel of the city's major radio and television stations, clinging to them as though it were her last chance. The political and bureaucratic tales she weaves to doormen, secretaries, and members of the press, are clearly just a thin step over the line of the compounded confusion and chaos that we all face. Unable to track me down by using her standard technique of calling at 5:00 PM and announcing that "they are breathing down my neck, my life is in danger, and I am exposed out on the street," she left an eight-page, single-spaced letter, parts of which are excerpted here:

Dear Miss Lamont:
Please come to my home to enterview me the week

*of September 3rd. Come any morning before 10:00
A,M, except for Wednesday, September 6, at which
time I am scheduled to attend an orientation for new
teachers entering into the public school system. There
has been a strong move by the City University to
prevent me from getting this position. . . . However, the potency of this move has its strong political,
bureaucratic, and political overtones which reaches
far beyond the City University.*

*The SEEK Program was disigned to pruchase all
books and supplies and other essentials that its students need, plus give funds for maintenance up-keep
according to an individual's needs. . . . However,
under Prof. CR's administration, once a student
reached the amount of $57.00 for books and supplies,
he was stopped from getting more books even if he
has no books for courses in which he was enrolled.
This Prof. place BC in charge of approving books
needed once the student reached $57.00. BC more
often than not is no where to be found. If we did
find him, he approved books for students that he
wanted to . . . refused other students regardless of
their financial situation. I took part of my rent money
to purchase the books. When time came for rent, I
had to take all of what I had left for food and car-
fare to school to pay the rent. After three days without eating . . . I took a student loan for $1,000.00.
From the $159.99 bi-weekly, I had to pay rent, buy
food, and run a complete house, i.e. pay light bills,
gas bills, phone bills, buy clothing, etc. My rent was
$116.50 with the new computing it is now $125.24
monthy.*

Then my SEEK stipend was cut by nearly seventy

dollars per month as a move to force me out of col-
lege. When this did not force me out of school I was
cut to $30.00 per week . . . and my student loan
refused. When I attempted to submit an application
for a New York State Loan they refused to accept my
application for this New York State Student Loan
unless I sign some fictitious papers that I had re-
ceived a National Defense Student Loan in the
amout of $500.00. . . . When this did not force me
out, they began to put "F's" on my senior year tran-
script. Although I am supposed to have been spon-
sored by SEEK, I am now $4,500 in debt to the
government and $3,000 or more in debt to instruc-
tors, students, friends, and relatives. Plus a restaurant
owner.

Finally the bureacracy reached the school where
I was doing my student teaching. . . . I was given
brooms and told to sweep the yard, transferred from
teacher to teacher & given an unsatisfactory report.
They held back several checks one was for $50.00
less than usual, and was from the City University in-
stead of the Board of Higher Education. My last
name was mispelled and they stapled the stub from
my check over this check in order that I would have
already signed before I knew that they had substituted
checks. When I saw this, I tried to get back the state-
ment that I had signed for $115.03 . . . they claim
they had deducted $50.00 I owed the school. I told
them to let me sign that I received $65.03 instead of
$115.03. After I threatened to bring the PRESS they
told me to sign that I received a check in the amount
of $65.03 and that fifty dollars was in part payment
of a loan I owed to them. Because of so much pres-

*sure and owing so many people, I thought it was
the City University that I owed $100.00 to but it was
someone else . . . after all. . . . The last day of
school a clerk in the change booth at 34th St tried
to get me to sell drugs for money. The Gas Company
in July turned off my gas for a bill I did not owe
them.*

*In November, the New York Telephone Company
turned off my phone for a bill I did not owe.*

*They blackmailed my brother who was in the
Army out of $24.00 by threatening to shut off my
lights one week before my finals. I told him I did not
owe the bill and he asked me about the New York
State Public Service Commission. I told him that all
of this was a retalitory act to force me out of school
because I called upon instructors, state agencies, private agencies, members of the Board of Higher Education, the Press, including politicians to survive, thus
the Public Service Commission would not help me.*

*I tried to prove I did not owe these bills, but my
bank statement was stolen. When I asked First National City Bank to forward me copies of two of
the checks and the bank statement, they claimed that
they could only send the front of the check, not the
back. . . . They finally deducted $4.50 from my
account and sent me blurry copies of two checks and
a statement which I did not order. They claim I failed
the Teachers examination by a little more than one
point . . . I am sure I passed, but do not have the
money to have the exam results pulled.*

*I have been followed and trailed heavily by both
Black and White in the summer after I sent several
letters to agencies and the Board of Higher Education*

requesting a $17.00 reimbursement for books and a flute that I had purchased for Music Class. The people who followed me range from their twenties to their sixties. They wore dungarees to white collars and closed in on me so . . . in such great numbers that I had to get students and instructors to help me escape in a cab. They asked me not to come home until I got it in writing. I put it in writing (the story) but this was stolen in my brother's car also. I stayed away from home and when I returned I learned that men had been here posing as detectives looking for me. Had I been here, Miss Lamont, I probably would have been dragged out of my apartment in the middle of the night arrested and falsely charged or perhaps they would have killed me. Barbara I must close here. Please come to see me. Don't write becuase it will definitely be picked up in the mail. My phone is disconnected so you can not call. I will just return home every day by six P.M. no matter what affairs I am taking care of the week of September 3rd. . . .

Exiled

You really can't manage to live on the West Side of Manhattan without becoming aware of the terrible political situation on the island of Haiti. In every subway station, fruit market, grocery shop, at every bargain counter, clusters of darkly distinctive people huddle, pattering rapidly in patois, clutching their exile proudly to them, foundering in the sea called Broadway.

Most of the non-French-speaking Americans in our neighborhood know that thousands of Haitians live here, but tend to think of them as just another group of immigrants who, like the West Indians and the German Jews, after a generation or two, will automatically absorb themselves into our culture. Most of my adult life I have known different.

Living in this cacophony I have come to understand patois almost as well as French. I have come to understand the true meaning of exile, the bitterness, hatred, oppression and fear, the suffering of families imprisoned, burned to death, or whose father just walked out one day never to return. The hotel ladies' rooms where Haitian doctors of philosophy, accountants, chemists, and lawyers clean the basins and dispose of dirty Kotex; the shivering in relentless winter winds; the fruitless search for a ripe plaintain. All these outrages assault me as I go about my business on Broadway, and one day I made the very simple decision to tell their story.

I started at the offices of the Haitian-American Service Center on Broadway at Ninety-sixth Street, where at 9:00 AM long lines of people seeking jobs begin to form. Most of the time, speaking not one word of English, these people are sent away jobless, only to return hopefully the following day. Mr. Jean Dupuis, the director, is a small, intense, bespectacled man, full of good will. I talked with a few people in French, listened to their incredible stories of being bused into factories for a dollar an hour, talked to laundrywomen old enough to be my great-great grandmothers, and joked with strong young men whose eyes were full of contempt and despair. After half an hour had passed, Mr. Dupuis called me into his office.

"I have just talked with Francois Benoit," he whispered, "and he has agreed to talk to you."

"Who is François Benoit?" I asked.

"A hero of the Resistance." He would say no more. We sat down to wait, and Benoit arrived shortly. He was a tall, well-built, handsome man but his face and eyes had a classic granite quality that reminded me suddenly of the Egyptian pyramids. At his suggestion, we went to a Haitian restaurant a few blocks away, and over a glass of watermelon juice, he unfolded his bizarre tale to me.

François Benoit was a young marksman in the Haitian army. In his early twenties he was already renowned, and when he captured a host of awards for marksmanship in the international games in Panama, he became a national hero. Soon after he returned from Panama, two expert marksmen picked off the personal bodyguard of President Duvalier's young son, but a kidnap attempt was foiled by other palace guards.

"I was on my way home to lunch," Benoit told me with a clear voice, speaking flawless English. "Just before I reached my house a servant came running, crying that soldiers had come and shot my eighteen-month-old son, my parents, and visiting friends. They had piled the bodies in the living room and burned down the house. All because it was said that only Benoit could pick off a guard at five hundred yards."

Benoit told me how he fled for his life to the Dominican embassy in Port-au-Prince, where he was to remain for seven years, a prisoner in his room. It was during this time that he taught himself English and chemistry. He later became a scientist, a chemical engineer in the USA. The Dominicans refused to surrender him to the Haitians, but eventually a deal was made, and seven years after his arrival there he was shipped out on a freighter late one night to take up residence in New York. Ironically, he seemed to feel that his new country was responsible, in large part, for the conditions he had fled from in Haiti.

"American companies own contracts for all the beef," he said bitterly. "Except for the very rich, meat is not to be had in Haiti, even though we raise much cattle. Power companies, sugar factories, all are leased to the Americans who pay us a dollar a day. And when the people try to have an uprising, the Americans send helicopters to support Papa Doc," he concluded.

I wanted to know if Benoit still kept in touch with what was happening in Haiti, and I asked him if conditions had changed under Duvalier Jr., popularly known as Bébé Doc.

"The man who led the troops that burned down my house and killed my family," he answered quietly, "has just been appointed the Haitian consul-general here in New York."

There are certain stories that lead you to talk aloud to yourself. I argued with myself that I should go and see the consul, then argued that it would be a great risk since a significant portion of the Haitian community knew about the interview; in fact, people were beginning to come up to me in the street. Afraid of the Haitian Secret Service, which remains active in New York, they would talk only in wide-open spaces. The Ton Ton Macoute made every anti-Duvalier Haitian look twice over his or her shoulder.

As in most other stories where I talk aloud to myself, my own total faith in my lack of paranoia saw me through. The next day I phoned the new consul-general for an interview. "Send us a letter," I was told by a Mr. Mehu, who, it turned out, had a child in my son's class at school.

In a detailed letter, I spelled out, both in French and English, the exact half-dozen questions I would ask. But the questions were very deliberately chosen and phrased. One read: "Is the original constitution still in effect?" This constitution was a guarantee of liberty and the pursuit of happiness, which I felt would bear exploring if I ever got to interview the consul-general in person.

A few weeks later I got the chance. A smartly uniformed chauffeur paid a visit to my television station, bringing me the personal greetings of Mr. Roger Lafontant, consul-general from Haiti, who had agreed to be interviewed under the specific conditions put forth in my letter. At nine o'clock one Wednesday morning I arrived at the Haitian Consular offices on East Forty-second Street, along with a camera man and a lights technician. I was shocked to see the guards wearing open arms—even in the worst days of confrontations with the Russians I had never seen unconcealed weapons in a diplomatic office. One guard carried hip pistols in a holster, swung a billy stick, and had handcuffs and a bullwhip hooked onto his belt.

We were ushered into a large office where Mr. Lafontant himself sat beaming from behind a huge mahogany desk. When my lights man moved a large leather sofa from against the wall, he found a pint of whiskey stashed behind it. The minute I saw the consul I knew I had him hooked. He was a large, corpulent, very black man, with a tendency to sweat and rock back and forth in his chair. I knew the camera would exaggerate these characteristics out of all proportion until he would appear extremely evil, but I had no inkling of how the questioning would go. After only a few questions things began to loosen up. Lafontant pulled out a private edition of *A Tribute to Martin Luther King,* by Francois Duvalier, President-for-Life of Haiti. He signed the book over to me as a gesture of good will between peoples.

"Do you mean to imply that Duvalier is a man of non-violence?" I asked suddenly. I'll never forget the way he folded his hands across his belly and continued to rock.

"Oh, you have to understand why we kill people in our revolution," he answered, smiling.

"Is that why you executed the Benoit family?" I pressed. A film of sweat appeared on the consul's forehead—he stammered, but didn't expressly deny Benoit's charges. He broke into French, explaining about honor and discipline. The cameras kept rolling, and I kept up a simultaneous translation of his answers, posing new questions in English. The intelligence man at his shoulder stood frozen as the man he'd been hired to watch over signed the death warrant to his career.

For weeks following the interview the Haitian consulate sent around armed chauffeurs with handwritten letters asking to see the film or for a text of the entire interview. After the station aired my interviews with Benoit and Lafontant back to back, I hear that bombs placed in Lafontant's car by Haitian militants had, on three separate occasions, failed to go off.

I should have known that wouldn't be the end of it. A few weeks later a Haitian man I knew knocked at my door; he asked me to step outside and have a private conversation with him on the Broadway mall. He assured me that it would be in my best interests.

"I have a friend who has a plan," he said once we were outside, "and would like very much to meet with you. Can you come to dinner next week at my house?"

When I arrived for dinner I met a tall, slender man who called himself simply Fleurival. Fleurival later came to my apartment and offered me fifty thousand dollars to go to Haiti and make a film favorable to the government, which no one would censor but he himself. He claimed to be a writer with film experience who couldn't go back to Haiti himself, but would like to see his country receive fair treatment in the press. I thought it best to draw up a long, involved proposal with an outrageous budget and impossible shooting terms, and indeed, after a few months went by, the whole matter was dropped. (My acquaintance and I still exchange politenesses when we meet and occasionally at Christmastime he brings us a bottle of Scotch.)

Some months after this I made the acquaintance of

Dr. Gaston Jumelle, a world-renowned gynecologist who heads the Charles Drew Medical Center in the slums of Brownsville. His brother, a candidate for president against Papa Doc, was brutally murdered in Haiti, and it is his coffin that is opened at high noon on the streets of Port-au-Prince in the movie *The Comedians*. Most of his family was killed or fled into exile. Jumelle is the acknowledged head of the Haitian exile movement, and out of our meetings came a suggestion for a meeting of Haitian leaders with the Black Congressional Caucus in Washington, which I helped to set up.

About fifteen or sixteen men and women, all leaders of the exile movement, arrived from different parts of the country, and I met them all in Washington's Union Station. As each was introduced to me I gradually became aware that most of them had brought bodyguards along. I took them to a borrowed apartment and left them alone with lots of liquor and potato chips; there they caucused for several hours before going on to the Congressional Office Building, where the Black Caucus had in turn invited the head of the Caribbean Desk at the United States State Department to be present. I have rarely felt so naked as I did following the bodyguards up those wide white steps to the meeting in the Congressional Office Building. Nothing untoward occurred, however, except for the most incredible meeting. The Haitians, so eloquent in French, couldn't get their story across at all in English.

There was one woman in the group who had come from New York City. Seven years before, her husband, an attorney who opposed the regime, had received a lunchtime visit from President Duvalier's personal guards. He left the house, never to return. For four years the Ton Ton Macoute visited her regularly, collecting money for her husband, who they said was in jail. Sometime during the fifth year, after having no direct word from him, she applied for an exit visa for herself and her four children, which was granted two years later. She is now convinced that her husband died the day he left home. When Papa Doc died, his son reported that there was never any record of the woman's husband being imprisoned anywhere on the island. She applied to the Red Cross, and at the meeting she appealed to the United States State Department to conduct an investigation. The State Department promised to make a request through official channels, but nothing more was ever heard.

The other members of the delegation made impassioned pleas in French, and I wound up acting as translator. They were asking the United States to investigate disappearances in Haiti, to look into the existence of alleged concentration camps, and to re-evaluate the United States' role of giving aid and military support to Duvalier. Another request was that Haitian refugees be given official refugee status like the Cubans—to this day the United States government refuses to admit that Haiti is a dictatorship and that three-fourths of all their educated manpower has fled the island for France, England, Canada, Africa, and the United States.

Shirley Chisholm and Charles Rangel asked some hard questions, which I thought the man from the State Department evaded nicely. He didn't have access to the exact amount of aid the United States gave, could only report that it had been cut under the Kennedy Administration. As for American helicopters, they were on the island to patrol Dominican borders, and, he said, "any reconnaissance flights over Haiti, especially in times of trouble, were designed to prevent an invasion from nearby Communist Cuba."

When we returned to New York, I did another lengthy

report for radio on the plight of the quarter of a million Haitians here. It was a less political series of reports, dealing with the everyday life of a permanent exile. Many Haitians can never return home because, in order to get away, they had to use an assumed name to obtain a passport. Once they got passports, these refugees entered the United States on visitors' visas and simply stayed on. Unlike Cuban refugees, however, who have been officially declared refugees and provided with well-funded multiservice centers and social and financial aid, the Haitian finds himself all alone.

In order to get refugee or exile status, these people would have to show a newspaper article proving that they were exiled, imprisoned, or persecuted in Haiti. Most of the refugees, however, never took part in a major revolt, and there is no publicity for those whose homes were simply visited in the night, and whose families were spirited away to jail or death.

Once here and speaking no English, they go to work as domestics or in factories, with English classes sometimes following later. But in the meantime they remain at the mercy of landlords, shopkeepers, and the prejudice accorded to blacks in America. Children are uprooted from one school system and placed in another, usually in a much lower grade. Those who can afford to, send their children to the French Lycée; another alternative is a public school on Manhattan's West Side that offers bilingual classes and curriculum similar to that of the Haitian system of education.

More than one half of the Haitian community is located in Brooklyn, where I met a young woman who typified the spirit of the Haitian exiles. She was in her early twenties, had a two-year-old baby in her arms, and had been out of Haiti for four years. She told me she had just gone back to school to study politics. Like most Haitians she spoke little English and was shy of the microphone.

"One day I'm going to return to my country. When this Duvalier government exists no longer, I'll go back to Haiti," she told me. "We all stay here a long time to earn money. When the government exists no longer, I'll go back to Haiti."

"And if the government doesn't change?"

"Well, it's only for a time," she told me. *"Il y a un temps pour rire et un temps pour pleurer."* There is a time to laugh and a time to cry. "What will I do there?" she shrugged. "That makes no difference, when the Duvalier government exists no longer I'm going back to Haiti. Yes, I will wait, but I get impatient. I hope one day the government will be no more," was all she could say.

"What are you doing now?" I asked, in an effort to draw her out. The light of the promised land was in her face as she replied, "I read, I go to school, I study, I wait. I don't even want to go to the movies. I will go back. *Je reviendrai."*

Bringing Home the War

Sitting on the subway on my way from one assignment in the Bronx to another in lower Manhattan, I pulled out some pamphlets the federal government had sent me earlier in the week. I had just been covering a story on drug addicts, so my attention was especially drawn to one pamphlet that read: "anyone can become addicted if he takes opiates regularly for a few weeks. However, certain kinds of people are more likely to become involved with heroin than others."

What kinds of people? I wondered. I would later find out that the pamphlet's anonymous authors were talking about veterans who, in ever-increasing numbers, were returning from Vietnam addicted to heroin, morphine, and barbiturates. I already knew that in 1971 the United States Army, Navy, and Air Force together discharged close to ten thousand clinically certified addicts and sent them back home. The government's widespread program of random urine testing only began in July 1972, however, and thousands of addicts had slipped through undetected. It was likely that thousands more would. In the beginning, my concern was not so much with the number of addicted veterans, but with the outrageous lack of services the government simply was not providing. In New York City, if a guy came back addicted, chances are he'd have an "undesirable" discharge, making it almost impossible for him to find work and making him ineligible for treatment at a VA hospital. It was largely as a result of my series and other exposés by members of the press that this policy was finally changed.

But on that subway train late one afternoon, I knew only that I wanted to find out what the government meant by "certain kinds of people." The next morning I went to see Roger Hurley, coordinator of New York City's Veterans Program Addictive Services Administration, who estimated the number of untreated veterans in New York City alone at thirty to forty thousand, with another thirty thousand in California. Hurley was bitter about the federal government's refusal to consider drug addiction a service-related disability—only four thousand veterans in the entire country were being treated by the federally run facilities for their habit.

"These men have done the job their country asked of them, they've been broken, brutalized, and mauled in the process," he said. "They returned to the United States with a habit that has been fed by ninety-eight percent pure heroin that was offered to them on the streets of Saigon and other cities and villages throughout Vietnam at the lowest possible price, within the means of the lowest enlisted man in the armed forces. Back in the United States, they're confronted with a debate as to whether or not anybody has any responsibility to them, as if the blood they shed in Vietnam was somehow different from the blood of men who fought in Korea or the second World War."

Hurley charged that nothing was being done to help veterans put their lives back together; to gain employment and re-enter society.

"They've been used," he concluded frankly.

According to both city and federal figures, while New York City programs were treating thirty-eight hundred drug users who were veterans, the Veterans Administration in the city only handled fourteen hundred. A confidential survey done by Louis Harris for the Veterans Administration in August 1971, listed admitted drug use among veterans after service. Two percent were heroin users, two percent opium, and one percent morphine addicts; a total of five percent were on hard drugs. The study showed another three percent to be using barbiturates, three percent amphetamines, and one percent methamphetamines. That added up to a total of twelve percent of all veterans admitting to being on addictive drugs. In addition, twenty-six percent of the veterans in the study admitted using other drugs, such as marijuana and LSD. A quick tally showed that out of six million Vietnam veterans, the hard drug population had to amount to some seven hundred thousand. And experts estimated that every returning veteran who was a drug addict would turn four friends into addicts as well. Drugs were being discovered coming into the United States in packages mailed by servicemen, and the drug plague was rapidly spreading into small towns as well as large cities. On paper the picture was sour, but I still had no gut feeling about the wave

of ex-servicemen pouring back into the cities with only an
overwhelming need for drugs to bolster them up.

I knew of a residential drug program called SERA
(Services and Education For Rehabilitation in Addiction)
in the Bronx, the only one in the entire city exclusively for
veterans, and one morning I went up there to talk to some
of the ninety-five guys in the house. Several young men
lounged on the run-down steps while others inside were
busy with hammer, nails, and bricks, renovating the entire
structure. Over the front doorway was a hastily painted
sign reading DMZ; the director explained that this meant
Drug Mending Zone. After being shown around the building, I settled on the front steps with a half dozen former
soldiers who, over the roar of passing trucks, told me their
stories. One of them, a young man named Adolphus, tried
to explain to me why people became addicted.

"You can't blame the drug problem on the home," he
said. "You find drugs in school; you find drugs on the street
—I mean, you find drugs when you go to work." His wide
smile grew even wider, and he swept his arm out in a
gesture that included the whole world. "Rich people, poor
people, black people, white people, any kind of religion,
you name it, and you got people using drugs, either smok-
ing or doping or dropping pills, you know what I mean?"

Then Adolphus told me something that I was to hear
again and again as I talked with veterans all over the city.

"The problem is the government," he said seriously.
"You know, they tolerate so much of it. You got countries
like Turkey, you know, that have been producing opium,
dope, for a long time, and then you got countries like Vietnam, Cambodia, Laos, Thailand—they're producing drugs.
That government tolerates it, you see? And then they ship
it over here." Most of the veterans I talked with felt that

the United States government could stop the heroin traffic, seventy percent of which originates in Southeast Asia, if it wanted to.

While some of the vets at the DMZ had been addicted before joining the service, the majority told me they picked up their habits overseas.

"When I was in the service for approximately nine months, I was wounded," one young man told me. There was an intense look in his dark eyes. "They sent me to the hospital and kept me there for about two or three days, and then they sent me back to the field. Well, during that time we were having pretty heavy maneuvers, and we were out practically every day, so what happened was my wounds got infected all over again. And at the time we didn't have that many people, you understand, to lead the squads and platoons and what not, so they kept me in there, and when the pain started to give me a lot of trouble, that was a problem on top of my other problems, and I needed a release. So I, you know, started using drugs."

"Were you out on the front line?" I asked.

"Yes, I was in the infantry."

"Where did you go to get drugs?"

"Where did I go?" he seemed confused. "I didn't have to go anyplace. I mean, they came to you. Like every day they would have someone coming in from NDP—that means night defensive position—and they would bring it in. Then the medics and the people that were staying back at the house would bring it out to the field. Just like that."

"What kinds of drugs were these?" I asked incredulously.

"Uh, heroin; then they had marijuana. Marijuana mostly at the time I was there. But not like you have grass here," he explained. "This stuff is strong, and you shoot up with it."

"What about barbiturates?"

"Barbiturates, pills, yes. They always had pills because a medic carries a lot of pills, morphine and things like that."

"What happened when you got into the Army?" I turned one step up to question a slender young man who looked to be about fourteen years old. He had long tapered fingers that drummed nervously on his pants leg.

"Well, I started with marijuana when I got over there, too, and then I started getting more with heroin, like when I started going to the field, I started getting it more easy. Like when you don't get mail, you start getting family problems, your sergeant's always behind you—all these little things get to you. And people that never been in a war, they don't like to be killing people. . . . I was trying to escape from that, from killing people."

"How many people did you have to kill over there?" I asked.

"I really didn't know, but I know I killed a lot, and I really feel sorry for them; it hurts me." He turned abruptly, picking up some tools, and re-entered the building; a twenty-two-year-old working desperately to rebuild a broken shell with bricks and mortar and wood, and thus perhaps to rebuild his own life.

Many servicemen never go abroad, but have drug habits they must feed right here at home. Benjy spent two years at Fort Dix, New Jersey. For the first seven months he would leave the base every night to buy drugs in Manhattan, returning at 5:00 AM the next morning. Then the strain caught up with him.

"I was working hard," he explained, "fifteen hours a day as a cook. We were short on cook time and I couldn't take the strain, so I went AWOL. I AWOLed twice, broke restrictions, and I was locked up. I made parole, I escaped, got caught, they put me back, and I told them I wanted a discharge right away. They didn't offer me no medical help of any kind."

Addicts in the AWOL category are not included in the general drug abuse statistics. Once an addict has gone AWOL he cannot get an honorable discharge, and this makes him ineligible for treatment by any VA hospital, no matter how long he has served. It was the same story again and again as I visited other programs for drug addicts and talked with veterans' groups at meetings and on street corners. They say they became addicted out of fear, frustration, loneliness, and to ease the pain of having to kill large numbers of people. Drugs were readily available in large quantities in South Vietnam, pills to be had without a prescription of any kind; heroin, marijuana, and cocaine were sold openly on the streets, and still are.

At this point in my investigations I wanted badly to talk to someone who could put some of the nightmare in perspective, so I went to see Frank Gracía, the director of SERA, who operates a gas station where the addicted veterans can work until they could get on their feet. I asked him what the government should do.

"Well," he said, shaking his neat mop of white hair, "some of the money that's going into methadone they should put into drug-free vocational rehabilitation centers, where veterans that don't know their rights can go and be helped with their pensions, schooling, or job placement. This kind of thing is what's needed, not just for addicted veterans, but for all veterans in general."

I went next to see the administrative assistant to the chief of staff at the Manhattan VA hospital, to ask why so few vets were being treated for drug addiction. He tried to explain that the hospital has many outpatient and in-patient programs to treat addicted veterans—but he didn't sound too convinced of his facts.

"We have a detoxification inpatient program where the addict is hospitalized for a period of fourteen days, and during this time, given decreasing doses of methadone so he is detoxified. Then there's the outpatient drug-free program, but this is usually a follow up to the inpatient one. Once a patient is drug-free he is followed up, coming in usually for an hour a day to receive group therapy."

Statistics show that less than ten percent of the veterans detoxified in this fashion stay off drugs for any length of time, and in any case a veteran with a general or undesirable discharge was ineligible, at that time, for help of any kind from the VA hospital. Several months later the government passed a regulation allowing a discharge to be reclassified if the only reason for an undesirable or bad conduct discharge was addiction, but this reclassification was hedged around with elaborate procedures, and no effort was made to reach out to the hundreds of thousands for whom it was too late.

The situation was not improved when, in the spring of 1970, the United States invaded Cambodia, opening up new trade routes for the shipment of heroin to South Vietnam. Of the more than nine thousand addicted veterans discharged in 1971, six thousand came out with general discharges. I called the Defense Department to find out what they considered their obligation to these veterans to be. The first barrier I ran into was their total rejection of the word "addict." "User is the official term," I was told. The Defense Department spokesman told a story in direct contradiction to that told by the men themselves.

"If a user shows up on the urinalysis, another test is

made of that sampling to make sure it was not a prescribed drug," he said. "The individual then is taken in for rehabilitation, and if it's severe enough he gets medical care, and hopefully within five to ten days dries out. Then the rehabilitation process starts as far as education goes. He sees his physician, he's talked to by counselors, and hopefully he becomes rehabilitated." Of the hundreds of veterans I talked with, not one had ever undergone this kind of process at the hands of the armed services.

"I told them that I was an addict and you know, they didn't do nothin' about it. They sent me to be detoxed, then they sent me back out to the field," said one of them to me.

"And you got hooked again?" I asked.

"Right. I got hooked right away and stayed hooked until I left."

"How did you leave? How did you get out finally?"

"I got hurt, and was in the hospital at Okinawa. When I got there, they knew that I was a drug addict; they detoxed me, then sent me to Camp Lejeune in North Carolina, where I was supposed to wait to get discharged. Instead of discharging me, they put me in the brig. And I stayed in the brig, under what they call an Article 32, for almost seven months. Then they gave me an undesirable discharge."

"For doing what?" I asked.

"For being a drug addict," was his answer.

The Defense Department admits that somewhere around three percent of all Vietnam veterans were also addicts. But this figure was contradicted by a former army captain who revealed that an unreleased report that he had helped to prepare for the army in 1971 showed a range of heroin use among soldiers between ten and forty-four percent.

Eric Engstrom, the retired captain, said the report was an attempt to warn senior officers of a time bomb that would explode in the United States. Apparently no one paid any attention.

There are a lot of guys like Adolphus and Calvin in the Bronx. Finding their problems in Vietnam echoed back home, unable to get medical treatment for their habits, unable to get jobs or enough federal money for a decent education, they return to drugs and just keep on taking a little bit more every day to ease the pain. And so the guys like José and Benjy sit on stoops in Akron, Milwaukee, and Los Angeles as well as the South Bronx, spreading the plague they can neither bring to a halt nor control, the plague that began with the heroin, cocaine, morphine, LSD, and high-grade marijuana shot into the veins of United States soldiers on the streets of Saigon and Pnomh Penh.

Bells and Bright Feathers

I really think the best radio series I've ever done was the one on the American Indian Power Movement. It all started with a man I'll call Joey, the Peruvian Indian who lived downstairs with a friend of mine—whom I'll call Harriet—whose Jewish parents thought she lived alone. Harriet left him to go live in Israel, taking her ten-year-old daughter with her. Joey, alone and distraught, took to picking up strangers and putting them up for the night. One evening he came by my apartment with Sandy Sandoval, a twenty-one-year-old Taos Indian from New Mexico.

Sandoval was eloquent about the beating his people were taking, on and off the reservations. As I listened I realized that I knew little if anything about the struggle of the native American for freedom, and so I was delighted when they invited me to a powwow at the McBurney YMCA on West Twenty-third Street. There is a powwow every month, they told me, open to the public, where you can meet some of the leaders of the Indian Power Movement, and have a good time dancing and chanting.

So one Saturday night I went down, and there indeed was a good old-fashoned powwow in full swing. There were brown, red, and yellow Indians, men, women, and little babies—and who should I find there but my old friend Gus the Jewish taxi driver from Brooklyn! There was so much chanting and bell ringing that I had to wait between dances to get my interviews, but after two hours I had talked to almost every major Indian leader in the country.

Philosophy, morality, and dignity seemed to govern their every thought and principle. Russell Means, who later went to jail—the case against him was ultimately dismissed—for incitement to riot, explained to me the sense of history passed down from generation to generation over the twenty-five thousand years since the original Indians crossed Alaska and entered the American continent, long before the Stone Age.

"The basic philosophy is that all living things, green things, rocks, four-legged things, winged things of the air, two-legged things, we all come from one mother, our mother the earth. That's why we were able to live here for twenty-five thousand years without raping or desecrating her in any way, shape, or form. 'Cause one doesn't rape his mother. The white man calls it ecology today," he sighed, "but to us it has a deeper and more spiritual meaning—to respect our Mother Earth."

Means pointed out that all the land now occupied by non-Indians was ceded at one time or another by Indian nations in return for services from the federal government. The services contracted for were primarily education, health aid, and help in economic development. But he was bitter about the exchange, since out of more than two billion acres of land, only sixty million remain in Indian hands.

"These services haven't been provided in any adequate measure whatsoever," he said flatly. "You name it, economics, housing, education, the American Indian is at the bottom of the heap. Our life expectancy is forty-four years of age, our infant mortality rate is two and one-half times the national average. And our teen-age suicide rate is ten times the national average. On and on."

Eddie Benton, a leader of the Indian Youth Movement, was also at the powwow, and he was even angrier. He shouted at me over the tinkling of bells.

"We have seen the white man and how he has acted, and we want no part of his lies, his deceit, his materialism. We don't want no part of that system. Just give us our culture and leave us alone. The federal government should live up to its agreements, and we will obey every law or submit to the penalty." He, like most of the Indians I talked with, considered himself a law-abiding conservative. His pride and anger had impressed me, and as I left the powwow, my head was swimming with all the music, bells, chants, and angry voices, all expressing the same frustration and desire for justice.

One of the major causes of this frustration is the United States government's land policy. The original Indian treaty of 1778 was basically a trade agreement: If the Indians gave up title to their land, the government would protect it from development or encroachment. But the present conflict arises because, while neither the government nor the

Indians can sell the land, Congress can and does appropriate it for public projects. Or so I was told by William Byler, a Caucasian who heads the Association of American Indian Affairs. As we sat in his tiny office crammed with Indianabilia, he explained that the Dawes Act of 1887 had carved up the reservations into 160-acre subdivisions, one to each Indian family on the reservation, which the Indians were then supposed to farm.

"The basic purpose behind the Dawes Act," he explained, "was to impel the Indian to become a farmer and husbandman. By so doing, the government hoped to turn him into a 'normal' American citizen. Then he would begin to think and behave like other Americans."

The Dawes Act didn't work. In a short time, fifty million acres were lost as the Indians couldn't amass enough capital to work the land. Much of this land was eventually given away in return for food for starving Indian families. One of the strongest rallying points at the powwow had been criticism of the government's efforts to relocate Indians away from their reservations. As Sandy Sandoval had said to me:

"They tell us we can join the army or go to college. But then you have to leave the reservation to get a job. They send you to these schools that don't relate to the Indian philosophy of life. For example, there's differences between jobs, jobs that are life-giving and the jobs that are not. There's jobs that give life to the planet, and there's jobs that take away from it. And these schools don't tell you that, don't try to put that into you." On the reservation, Sandoval said, "you can learn from somebody who knows you, like maybe a grandfather or your uncle. Somebody could tell you things; that's the way you learn."

My research showed that close to half a million Indians live on reservations today, another half million have been relocated by the federal government to eight major cities. Although those Indians living on reservations no longer need permission each time they leave the reservation, there is nowhere to go. Little or no industry exists on reservations, and most schools, health services, and trading posts are run by whites. As Russell Means had told me:

"There's a brain drain on the reservation. Because of a lack of opportunity, the young people have to leave in order to get a full stomach." Means felt that relocation should be replaced by a program of manpower training on the reservations. In this way Indian leadership could be built up indigenously.

"The goal of the United States government is cultural genocide of a people," he said bitterly, " 'cause once a people lose their culture they turn into facsimile white people."

The picture Means painted of Indian life out West was a grim one. A young Indian man just out of school may commute one hundred miles a day to the nearest city to work, often finding an unwelcome reception. The only job where the Indian has traditionally held a monopoly is, of all things, construction work on high bridges and skyscrapers. The Indian steeplejack is so much a part of the white man's mythology about his red brothers that I felt my story wouldn't be complete unless I talked to one of the old chiefs in the construction trades.

So one Monday morning I took the subway to Livingston Street in Brooklyn where I found the home of Paul Horn, a Mohawk from Canada. I climbed to the second floor to a small apartment filled with Indian fur boots and other hand-crafted items and introduced myself to Horn, an imposing figure with a bulbous nose and erect carriage. The story passed on for generations among white builders was that Indians, because of their mountain experience, are more sure-footed and better suited for work high above the ground. Paul Horn scoffed at that.

"It's a trade that we didn't have to go to high school for," he explained. "A trade that brought you quick money and challenged your ability to show that you were not afraid of heights." Horn told me that when Indian fathers and uncles would come back to the reservation with the high pay they earned in the construction business, boys of fifteen and sixteen would try to emulate them and start training early, so that when they became trade trainees at twenty-two or twenty-three years of age, they already had six years on their Caucasian counterparts. Despite his cynicism, Horn was genuinely proud of his many years as a bridge builder and proud of the many structures, including the Brooklyn Bridge, on which he'd worked. And yet closeted in his tiny house with the Indian handicrafts and memories of his home tribe, he seemed fearful of what he and others in the Indian movement feel is a governmental termination policy aimed at liquidation of their trust lands and, eventually, of their people and entire culture.

"We don't want to be culturally emasculated," I heard over and over again.

One symbol of this termination policy was, to Indians, the takeover of the sacred Hopi Black Mesa by power companies. The companies promised the Indians that it would create jobs, but it didn't.

"To get the coal from Black Mesa to the power plant, you have to have a slurry line," Sandy Sandoval told me, "and a slurry line is fifty percent coal and fifty percent water. Now all of the water in New Mexico is very precious, and they get this slurry line, and it just wastes water full of all that coal. This one power plant puts out the same amount of pollution as Los Angeles and New York on the same day. The smoke cloud is about two hundred miles long and you can see it all the way from Sante Fe."

Power plants promising jobs and then polluting the air, lumber companies bulldozing forests instead of cutting down trees selectively—these were the things the Indians spoke out against. "We are fighting for our culture," Russell Means concluded. "You see, we are a non-competitive people in the sense of the white man. We don't want to become the foreman, the office manager, the vice president, the congressman. All we ever wanted was a full stomach and an adequate shelter and the means to provide them." In his view, this was not a militant or radical position, but a conservative one—but whatever it was, Means ended up in jail and the Indian Power Movement went underground, many of its leaders hunted by the FBI. Before this happened they had carried their struggle—to control their own destiny by controlling their own education, developing cottage industries, clearing their land and beaches, and building up what they called "life-giving co-operative projects" —to communities across the nation. They left their mark on me as well: I often think of the powwow at the Mc-Burney "Y" and the incessant sounds of bells, the bright feathers and pipes, and the dignity of these people fighting for survival in what was once their country, stretching, as the song said long ago, "from sea to shining sea."

PART IV

Mrs. Madison of Tompkins Avenue in Brooklyn lived in a shoe; she had so many children she didn't know what to do. Actually, it was only eight and two grandchildren; her husband didn't count—he was a bedridden alcoholic. Mrs. Madison (that's not her name, but it's what I call her) knew all about corruption, which meant vagrants living in the empty house next door, junkies breaking into her basement, city workers stealing pipes, building inspectors with their hands out, and cops coming by on holidays.

Mrs. Madison had saved up to buy her house in 1960 for eighteen thousand dollars. She rented the storefront to a Holiness church and kept two floors for herself. The top floor leaked, but brought in a small income. She tried never to go on welfare. She clothed her sons and daughters and sent them to school in Flatbush, feeling very rewarded when they won prizes and kept off the streets after dark. Of course, her two oldest girls brought home babies, but what else was she there for? She nursed the babies and sent the girls back to college. But something was missing.

If she had two thousand dollars she could put in locks and burglar alarms and make her house penetration proof. Only the city could get in with their Model Cities program to tear it down. She called me at my radio station every week for a year to say that if only she had a job typing envelopes, she could pay for college books for the kids. Welfare finally lent her money, but took a third mortgage on the house in return.

The Rent Control Board ruled that because she'd neglected to file for a rent increase two years previously, the top floor tenant could live for a year, rent-free. Then Welfare told her to sell the house, and they would pay five hundred a month for rent somewhere else.

Her girls had no nice clothes, but one day a salesman came around offering to make her oldest a stewardess, for only eighty dollars down. Mrs. Madison's endurance lies in her knowledge that as long as the babies keep coming, no one can ever take them away from her. And before she dies, maybe one out of the ten will survive to become rich or famous, or even just a huge success.

This Building Is Condemned

I will never forget my first television assignment in New York. I was to interview Chief Red Fox, a self-proclaimed one-hundred-and-eight-year-old Indian chief who, it later turned out, had faked his autobiography and was really only ninety-six or ninety-seven years old. When I got to his small suite at the Algonquin Hotel in the West Forties, he was seated by the window in full headdress. I had a couple of written questions about his book, but the only things I remember are trying not to breathe too loud into the mike hung around my neck, and his confiding that he had reached such a ripe old age because he ate no meat, only fish and vegetables.

My first assignment for all-news radio began somewhat less spectacularly. I was turned loose in the city and told I had only seven hours to hand in a four-part series on some issue concerning the local community. My political background came in handy. I simply called all my district leader friends and chatted for a few minutes about their problems. I was especially interested in one Brooklyn politician's tale of a group of old West Indian ladies who had gathered together to prevent the destruction of a hundred-year-old tree. The proverbial bulb lit up over my head and I could hear in my imagination the lilting tones of the Caribbean and the soft Southern dialects, the whisper of palm-fronds and the sound of the breeze in the Spanish moss. I loved it.

So, having called the group's leader, Mrs. Ruth Shannon, for an appointment, I set off early one morning on the subway with my tape recorder. In Brooklyn I was served tea in fragile cups on the basement level where the ladies had gathered. It was 10:00 AM and I had to turn in the completed tapes, cut and edited, by 5:00 PM. I felt like a long distance runner pacing out the laps.

As luck would have it, the women were articulate and candid—and the picture of the hundred-year-old tree threatened by modern progress gave way to a grimmer one of block after residential block being threatened by mass demolition to make way for buildings of the new Model Cities program. The bulldozers were coming through and the women had tales of families being deliberately burned out or vandalized to force them to move. In short, the tree might be saved, but the houses around it and the lives they encompassed were coming down.

When I left the women, I called another political friend who gave me a brief tour of most of the renovation area, and then drove me back to Manhattan. Three and one-half hours had elapsed since I set out. Back at the station I hurriedly cut out all but those pieces of tape that told the story quickly and succinctly, wrote a few "wraps" around the tape, tied the parts together, and five minutes before the deadline, presented myself to my editor. I have since realized that he didn't think I could do it.

Half a year later I went back to Brooklyn, remembering the old women, and began a series of reports on the programs of the Model Cities Administration, which eventually took me to all the boroughs and across to Hoboken, New Jersey, and won the Associated Press Award for excellence in journalism.

It all began with Horace Morancie, who had a steel band back in the early sixties and collaborated with my husband to produce some Calypso concerts that lost a lot of money. A few short years later, Horace had become director of the Central Brooklyn Model Cities Administration programs. He was delighted to see me again and talked freely about his powers, which he described as, "Planning, monitoring, and evaluating." The words cropped up with regularity, every five minutes, just like the chorus of a song.

"The idea behind Model Cities programs, as we see it," he said, "was to bring basic authority and control for the development of an area, or rather the funds that come into an area—particularly, federal funds—under the office of the mayor. If you check, you will see that most of your mayors had no hand in how much money was coming into their areas. And even worse, they had very little control over how that money was spent."

Morancie told me that although a large percentage of the sixty-five million dollars they received originally was spent on supplementing neighborhood services; the bulk of the housing, health, and education facilities was funded by a combination of city, state, federal, and private sources.

In other words, Model Cities agencies acted as contractors for community services. The Housing and Development Administration was the city's operating agency for relocation and emergency repair programs; the Board of Education operated educational information centers and bus trips; and the Economic Development Administration operated a program for vest-pocket industrial renewal. At the same time, community residents were supposed to have a say in this overall planning, monitoring, and evaluating process. However, once funds were allocated to the operating agency, they left the control of Model Cities. Morancie, later replying to charges of irregularities leveled by a local newspaper, was to say, "There is little financial management at this end; therefore, little to mismanage."

In short, Model Cities funds simply provided the seed money to encourage other private and governmental agencies to acquire heavy funding from the government, to operate programs that Model Cities would then oversee.

The problem in 1966–67 was that, with Model Cities being funded as a five-year plan, the City went ahead and appropriated money to demolish houses on a wide scale. The Brownsville section of Brooklyn still resembles post-World War II Germany, and Morancie tells me that most of the housing plans are still on the drawing board. For although the money to tear down buildings was allotted in 1966, architects were not hired until 1969, when construction money actually became available. In the meantime, the community was up in arms. Private homeowners saw groups of ministers, politicians, builders, and speculators coming into their neighborhoods, incorporating, and becoming sponsors of subsidized housing, yet they were told that they couldn't incorporate and do likewise to save their own homes.

Half of the proposed housing in the Central Brooklyn Model Cities area was to be low-income subsidized housing, renting for twenty-five to thirty-five dollars a room. There were two kinds of sponsors for these planned buildings: non-profit sponsors and limited dividend sponsors. But the limited dividend investor, whose profits are limited, received big tax benefits for sponsoring such housing. In addition, a limited dividend sponsor could retain control of the buildings until this tax shelter expired, a period of up to ten years. Sometimes these builders also got a packaging or developer's fee.

Upon further investigation, I found that the New York City Real Estate Department had some highly questionable methods of condemnation. They were not required to notify the homeowner of intent to condemn their property. A number of court decisions in the early nineteen-fifties had ruled that "Urban Renewal is a valid public purpose for which the government may make use of the right of eminent domain to acquire private property." On the rare occasions when, masquerading as a student, I got access to the City Planning Commission's files, I would see entire blocks mapped out for demolition and scheduled to be replaced with middle-income developments. Yet the houses were still standing, their owners blissfully ignorant of the plans downtown.

Early one morning I went to interview Daniel Bayer, director of the Department of Evaluation and Acquisition. It had taken me three weeks to zero in on this little-known department that makes most of the painful decisions about condemnation of property. I asked Bayer how the decision to condemn large areas comes about.

"Well," he said, rocking back and forth in a large chair behind an even larger solid oak desk, "you first have to

establish the legal public use or purpose. The urban renewal plan is submitted to the Planning Commission for
public hearing and decision to say that yes, this is a good
plan and should be effectuated. After that, you go to the
Board of Estimate for a resolution, first approving the
plan, and then authorizing you to take this piece of land
and put a school here, housing there. The City sends out
an appraiser, then goes to court and takes title to the
house." He smiled.

"Is this done without the homeowner ever being notified?" I asked.

"There's no point in pushing people out until the
architectural plans are ready," said Bayer, "until you've
gotten your building permit, that sort of thing. There's no
point in emptying out the land and then just leaving it
there unused," he concluded.

Yet that's exactly what happened in Brooklyn. Miles
and miles of slums were reduced to wasteland; a few trail-
ers were put up for "temporary housing," at a cost of
fifteen thousand dollars each, and are still there five years
later. This fifteen thousand dollar figure included the cost
of laying a foundation, sewage, gas, and electric lines, as
well as landscaping. However, the cost of building a single
unit of regular housing was estimated at thirty-nine thousand dollars.

And block after block was demolished.

I interviewed Mrs. Levi Sills over her front fence, with
inquisitive garbage men stopping off to listen in on the
conversation.

"My husband remodeled from top to bottom," she
cried, "every room in my house: the basement is finished,
closets built into the wall, my son's closets, my daughter's
closets, and things built right into the wall. . . ." Here

she broke down, but after a moment continued shakily, "We worked every night, he and I together. We laid cement on the floor just by ourselves with pieces of wood we slid across. They came and told me that week that they was taking over this property along here and that we was to be considered tenants. So I asked them how they figured that, and they said this is the way the city works. So they told us we had to pay rent; so I asked him how they figured our rent, and he said according to our room. He said my tenant would have to pay ninety dollars, and we would have to pay a hundred and fifteen."

Mrs. Sills asked the man from the city how they'd figured that, when the Sills' were renting units to two families, and all three families were living there at a cost of one hundred dollars a month.

"I don't have nothin' to do with this, lady," the man from the city said after she told him she wouldn't pay rent until she got a bill. When the bill finally arrived two or three months later, arrears had piled up and the Sills' had to pay some four hundred dollars in back rent. For two years they paid rent without receiving any cash payment for the purchase of their home, which seemed strange to me. I asked Bayer by phone why the Sills were asked to pay rent.

"In theory we, the city, are now the owners," he responded promptly. "If the tenant doesn't want to pay rent, but is going to stay on for six months or so, our management division will work up a deal whereby he can charge his rent against his ultimate award for the house."

The amount of the award is based solely on the city's appraisal of the property, and the actual payment can take up to four years if the owner decides to take the city to court. There is a special condemnation court, and when the city decides to acquire property, the Corporation Counsel of the City's Law Department petitions the court, saying only that the city needs the land for public improvement. The judge signs the order and the city takes title to the house—often without the knowledge of the owner.

When an owner retains an attorney, it is not unusual for a house having a market value of twenty thousand dollars to be appraised at ten thousand, with the judge finally setting a compromise award at fifteen thousand. If the owner happens to have a fifteen thousand dollar mortgage on the property, he is stuck. The situation gets even more complicated because the city only pays six percent interest. If the city doesn't pay the purchase money for twelve months, the owner loses the difference between his mortgage interest and the city's interest rate. Then in order to collect his or her first advance payment, the homeowner may have to hire a lawyer, who will charge up to eight or ten percent of the total. Time and time again in the Central Brooklyn Model Cities program I found that the owners, usually little old ladies, got neither enough to make a down payment on a new house nor enough to pay the security, agency fee, and advance rent required on an apartment.

One of these little old ladies was seventy-year-old Louise Boyd, who had owned her nine-room brownstone on Green Avenue since 1946. She was suddenly informed that the city now owned her house and was going to tear it down for a school. Appraisers and relocation agents came in, and a year later, she got the sum of eight thousand dollars, but the worst was yet to begin.

"Two weeks after the Relocation and Real Estate people went away," she told me, "vandals started breaking into the house. I didn't feel like staying there 'cause I was afraid. They tore out all the pipes, the toilet, the basin, and took all the stoves, tables, furniture; they even destroyed all my clothing."

Mrs. Boyd led me into the house, which was a total shambles. Locks had been broken, windows and doors smashed, old hats and shoes were burned, and hypodermic syringes with bloody cotton lay amidst the debris next to handwritten letters from the early twenties and smashed china and stemware.

"I went to the police at first," she said. "They say, 'well, when a house is condemned, what do you expect?'" In front of my news camera, she began to cry. "I don't know what I'm going to do. I don't want to go on welfare when this little money is finished. That's the reason why I used to go without even a new dress, to save a dollar so that when my husband and I got old we could have a place to call home, rent a few rooms out, keep us from welfare. Now he's dead three years; I'm all alone. We put off having children just to pay for a decent place we could call our own." She stumbled and sat down in the rubble. "After living here twenty-six years and calling it home, then within two months everything you have is gone."

Often while I was following this story in the Brooklyn Model Cities area, my film crew and I would become aware that we were being carefully watched. Sometimes a car with two men would idle at the curb, making enough noise by gunning their motor to ruin our sound track. Or the police would walk by and the homeowners fall silent. Tenants told tales of men who came in the middle of the night, broke into the houses, and yelled at the top of their voices to frighten residents. And then there was the weird pattern of fires.

On almost every block, a few weeks after the first few condemnations, a strategic building would suddenly burn down. Vandals looting the burned out building would spread to other houses, making the whole block practically uninhabitable. Sometimes the corner buildings would burn down; in other instances it would be houses in the middle of the block; and other homeowners would soon have to move. The people who were left bought dogs and built high fences when theirs was the only house left in a block of vacant lots. One man, who didn't want to be identified, told me, "They're a bunch of gangsters, hired and paid with Model Cities money who go around setting homes on fire, breaking in, going down to the basement to destroy your boiler so it costs too much to repair. They'll take a toilet and crack it so it can't be used. This is not thieves doing this; somebody's doing this to harass the people to make them move."

A check with the Fire Department revealed an incredible arson rate. "It's not kids setting these fires," one chief told me. "These are pros who want to steal pipes, copper tubing, and fixtures. They want to chase the people out."

There is, however, nowhere they can move to—not in the neighborhood, anyway. In 1971, the federal Department of Housing and Urban Development declared a moratorium on acquisition and demolition until an acceptable relocation plan was developed. In the meantime, only a few scattered housing developments had actually been built, and tenants complained that while they paid money under the table to get these new apartments, many were told months later that the units had already been rented to someone else. And there weren't enough units to go around.

When asked, Model Cities spokesmen point out that

increasing the number of housing units in the target area
was never a goal. "Our major concern is with improving
the quality of housing and neighborhood services in general," I was told all over the city. On one sample tract I
examined in the Bedford-Stuyvesant section of Brooklyn,
the 1970 census showed sixteen hundred and one housing
units. Only three hundred twenty-six were scheduled to
take their place. The Fulton Park area, which had con-
tained twenty-three hundred units, was scheduled for
eighteen hundred new units, which included townhouses
priced around forty thousand dollars.

These plans for the future were detailed in a wealth of
books commissioned by the Model Cities corporation to
describe their programs—books that were so heavy I
couldn't even lift them onto my desk. Complete with
glossy photographs of bright young people living in brand
new housing complexes, the books explained where the
more than four hundred million dollars went in New York
City Model Cities. The fine print spelled out Model Cities'
primary goals: "to reorder inconsistent land use patterns
and to cope with problems which cause deterioration and
blight." No deterioration or blight was pictured in these
weighty tomes. In the end, Morancie said it all.

"Every city needs a Model Cities process. The process
of having an agency responsible for planning, monitoring, and evaluating puts that agency in a position where
you're not in the day-to-day operation of things. You can
really stand back and look at the way things are going and
work on changes; work on innovation." I wondered if
Mrs. Sills and Mrs. Boyd would agree.

Little Miss Muffet Lives in the South Bronx

Some of my best stories come to me from unlikely sources like the United States Postal Service, and one such story, though I didn't know it at the time, started the day I received a letter from the Reverend Mrs. Catherine Pointer asking me to come and see her and broadcast her plight to the world. She owned two large houses in the South Bronx, including a small ground floor church on a half block in the Bronx Model Cities area.

The Bronx Model Cities neighborhood covers fifteen hundred acres and houses some quarter of a million people, sixty percent of whom are Puerto Rican, thirty-five percent black, and the remainder white. Despite ethnic differences, they all share the same substandard housing and high rate of crime. All suffer from a high incidence of fire and decaying conditions that the Model Cities brochures say have overwhelmed the neighborhood. The 1966 Model

Cities program in the South Bronx, coming on the heels of failing nineteen-sixties federal housing programs, was supposed to create a locally initiated strategy and full citizen participation.

The demolition there didn't begin until 1969 and—as was not the case in Brooklyn—there were few one- and two-family homeowners to be evicted. The majority of residents in the area lived in tenements and had to be relocated, a process which took some time.

On the day I arrived two bulldozers were approaching the Reverend Mrs. Pointer's three-story white frame house from different directions; and the rest of the block had already been razed. Yet abandoned vacant structures stood untouched on the next block. A mangy white dog sniffed at the padlock on the gate and howled in tune with the roar of the bulldozers as I rang the bell. Reverend Pointer, a small, dark brown, sharp-eyed woman with a cheerful smile, let me in, and we walked to the back of the church to escape the deafening noise. There she told me a story that made me think little Miss Muffet had suddenly come to life in the South Bronx.

Reverend Pointer had some large envelopes full of back correspondence. On July 25, 1970, she got a letter from Model Cities dated July 15, inviting her to a Board of Estimate hearing to be held the morning of July 23. The hearing had taken place two days before she got the letter, which read, in part, "A committee has been elected to represent you in preparing a Model Cities plan to improve our community. Your building is on one of the planned sites and you are welcome to attend the hearing. If the plan is approved you'll be notified. This is not a notice to move"; the letter went on, "in fact, you should not move. You are entitled to help in relocating."

Mrs. Pointer had no intention of moving. Instead she wanted to build a complex to house senior citizens on the site, to accommodate some of the tenants she currently housed in her two buildings. She argued that some of her roomers had heart conditions; others had just been released from mental institutions, and as long as they lived with her they didn't have to worry about being harassed by strangers.

On July 30, the Reverend Pointer got another letter signed by a Mr. Krakow of the Bronx development office, which referred to the rest of her property. "Mention of Block # 2632, lots 17 and 20 was inadvertently omitted from the original letter sent you by Model Cities," it read. "I believe your organization owns these properties as well, which are now a part of larger site 102. The South Bronx Neighborhood Development Plan, the official document which authorizes the city to acquire your property, has already received approval of the City Planning Commission and the Board of Estimate." The letter continued, "The city will take over your property some time after January 1, 1971."

Mrs. Pointer countered by going to an architect and a bank for help.

"I have a certain amount of money for a building fund," she told me. In fact, after a little coaxing she admitted that although the church nominally owned the property, her daughter held the mortgage, so in effect she had clear title to the land.

"We have a bank behind us who's willing to lend money to build this project; and we have our construction engineer's architect; he's willing to give seed money to build it," she reported. "He's ready; he wants to, and he's asking us to straighten out the title so that he can do it." She wrote letters to the city, but all the replies directed her to Model Cities Director Victor Marrero, saying that her property was now part of his target site.

It was not until February 11, 1971 that the city officially took over her property, and although all correspondence had told Mrs. Pointer specifically not to move, the city now demanded back rent from July. In November 1971, the city went to court, and based on affidavits signed by two city appraisers whom Mrs. Pointer refused to admit to inspect her property, got a judgment ordering her to pay $250 a month in rent, plus $2,410.71 in back rent accumulated from the time the city officially took over her property until June 1972. When Mrs. Pointer went to see Marrero, he told her to talk to Albert Goodman of the One Hundred and Sixty-third Street Improvement Council, a subsidiary of the local Morrisania anti-poverty agency. But Mr. Goodman, as it turned out, had already been designated as co-sponsor to build five hundred and fifty housing units on the very site where Mrs. Pointer had her home.

After Mrs. Pointer had briefed me on all these Byzantine goings-on, I left the church and went over to the Model Cities office where I had an appointment with Vincent Marrero. He was most unhappy to find out that I was there about the Pointer property. "She has no community credentials," he argued. "We had never heard of Reverend Pointer until she heard that the property was going to be taken."

"Was it then too late for her to become a sponsor?" I asked.

"Yes, it's too late," he explained. "Part of the thing is complicated, you see, because she doesn't want to move. She feels that the government has no right taking her little property away, and also that whatever housing is built on the property should be sponsored by her church. From where I sit," he said, "it's really quite unreasonable on more than one score."

I asked Marrero how the sponsors had been chosen, and here he seemed to be on comfortable ground . . .

"Sponsorship is really something you don't advertise for," he said. "You really can't go around the neighborhood saying all the people interested in sponsoring, you know, come on in. Sponsorship is a matter of organizations that are already established and have the capacity, the know-how to follow up, to hustle, in effect."

Once the Model Cities Policy Council approved certain sponsors, it appeared, these sponsors received federal money to build limited profit housing. After doing my homework I discovered that Albert Goodman, as well as several other sponsors, were members of the very same Model Cities Policy Council that had recommended them as sponsors. The same people were also turning out to be heads of anti-poverty agencies, commonly called community corporations.

The day after my talk with Marrero I returned to the Bronx to talk to Goodman. The One Hundred and Sixty-third Street Improvement Association, a storefront under the elevated train line, was full of desks and files and people who grew silent as I walked in. Groups of men who were leaning on desks disappeared, and Goodman's secretary frowned at me in disapproval. Goodman himself was a big, burly character who led me into a back office and showed me to a folding chair. I moved right in across the desk with my microphone and began to ask some hard questions. Goodman said he had no dialogue with the Reverend Mrs. Pointer.

"We have gone repeatedly out and asked Mrs. Pointer to work with us," he said brusquely. "When anyone thinks that they are greater or they are above working with other grass-root people, then you have no dialogue." I asked Goodman how he had become the sponsor of Mrs. Pointer's property.

"Our organization went before the Morrisania local committee," he explained. "They in turn carried it to the main policy committee of the South Bronx Model Cities program, and from there it went down to the central Model Cities office. I guess somewhere in between manipulations we were granted the sponsorship of a site in Model Cities."

Reverend Pointer, realizing how such decisions were made, had tried to run for the policy council, so she could have a say in who would sponsor her property. But she couldn't even find out when and where the election was being held.

"I call; I go down; they won't even tell me where the people have to register to vote," she told me. "The night before the election I went down to get my material, and I told them again that the people want to know and I don't know where to tell them." Mrs. Pointer complained of voting irregularities, people campaigning right inside the school where the voting went on, helping voters to pull down levers. But in spite of everything, she lost by only a single vote. Several policy council elections were subsequently overturned because of irregularities, but Mrs. Pointer's wasn't among them.

This story of old-time politics in modern urban renewal cried out for further investigation. In the church Mrs. Pointer had given me names of individuals who would back up her story, and I now went to work tracking them down. After much trying, I finally reached one of these people, William Shuller, on the phone. Shuller explained that he, too, had run for the policy council.

"I asked a lot of questions and got a couple of phony

answers, so I figured I'd run for the Board and see what's happenin'," he told me. "But they didn't want me to run. I had a big mouth."

"Did anyone discourage you from running?" I wanted to know.

"Well, you know, they'd say I'm not gonna win, and they called down to the mayor's office where I used to work and told them that I was splitting the black community. And then," he paused impressively, "John Mudd, of the mayor's office, gave me a strong warning. He said, 'I suggest you pull out of the race or,' in so many words, lose your job." Incredulous, I asked what happened next, and learned that Shuller had, in fact, pulled out of the race.

It was about this time that the Reverend Mrs. Pointer began to be harassed by organized groups of teenagers who started breaking her windows.

"We had to lock everything; we had to put gates on the outside to keep them from getting up on the porch, and then, when they found the gate locked, they come and twisted the bars and tore the gates up so you can't pull them together," she said. "When the police would come, they would get on the other side of the street and jeer at the policemen, and as soon as the police get out of sight, they come right back here again."

"You had none of this before 1970?" I asked.

"No, it hadn't been like that. Oh, once in a while you got a window broken, and like that, but nothing else."

I asked if she thought the harassment was deliberate.

"I believe these boys are being instructed or paid," she said, "because of something I saw in a meeting in a church, somewhere around Franklin Avenue. I went to find out what was going on . . . how someone was elected to represent me before the Planning Board, before the Board of Estimate. . . . As though we can't represent ourselves." She was outraged. "So I went to this here meeting and saw a group of those same boys that had set on this here stoop and stoned my house."

"Who sponsored the meeting?" I asked.

"Ah, they call it the Coalition, there was two people there that I knew, Albert Goodman and a woman who is another sponsor. They was speaking concerning running for the Model Cities."

Mr. Goodman later admitted that he did send kids around to see Mrs. Pointer, but only to give her leaflets. He says she cursed them away.

"We have what we call a neighborhood youth corps, and these are the kids we utilized to carry out leaflets in the neighborhood, to disseminate the information that we have to get out to the people," he said portentously. I asked Goodman if he was aware that Mrs. Pointer was terrified of these kids he sent out.

"I don't believe Mrs. Pointer is no more afraid of those kids than she's afraid of the other kids that she cursed out and runs away from her building, or the adults that she runs away from her buildings," Goodman replied. He was getting angrier by the minute, and I saw no point in staying.

Visits from window-breaking boys were not the only horrors Mrs. Pointer had to contemplate. She mentioned a young man who, she said, was investigating the Model Cities program.

"He told me some very hairy tales that had happened to people when they insist on doing something that the group don't want them to do," she said, her voice trembling.

"What kinds of things?" I asked unashamedly.

"Well—" she hesitated. "Drastic things. He told me for example, about a car running off the street onto the sidewalk and killing somebody, and some of this and some of that. So you may come up missing." She leaned more closely toward me and whispered in my ear, "And you know the black cop they just indicted up here? He's the one that used to come by my house every Christmas, and I used to pay him off."

One of the Reverend Mrs. Pointer's improbable stories checked out. The hit-and-run incident occurred in August 1969, when a young anti-poverty worker was pushed in front of a car and killed. The incident was reported to have occurred following a dispute between two local anti-poverty groups over control of Model Cities funds. Three members of one agency were charged with first-degree murder, but a grand jury later dismissed the case. That particular agency has since received over eleven million dollars in funds, and in 1970, one and one-half of those millions was found to be unaccounted for.

The stated goal of the South Bronx Model Cities program, like that in Brooklyn, was "to give positive direction to future assaults on urban blight in American cities." But construction ran into major problems because of soaring building costs. The only building that went through without too much trouble, was public housing. Model Cities in the Bronx had created a special housing corporation whose job it was to provide seed money and offer technical housing assistance to local sponsors. This corporation got two million dollars the first year and three million the second year.

Day care centers, adult education classes, and drug rehabilitation programs also got Model Cities funds. But the life of the South Bronx resident didn't undergo any significant changes. The fires, fear, and harassment remain, and all of Model Cities efforts did not produce enough jobs, decent housing, parks, schools, or a lower crime rate. Albert Goodman's parting words to me were bitter.

"Moderate-income housing in New York City has been a farce," he said, "because of the high cost of construction. It can work maybe in a small town in Ohio or a small town out West, but the construction unions and cost of materials in New York City keep us from realistically building substantial moderate-income housing here."

As I left Goodman's office I was followed by a slight, mustachioed man and another darker, more heavy set type. After two cabs and the "D" train the mustachioed gent was still with me, and it was not until I had gone through a series of complicated little maneuvers that I was able to make my way home without a tail. I never checked to see if they were employees of any of the rival Model Cities groups. I just accepted this fact of life as another part of the complex struggle for survival in the jungle called the South Bronx.

PART V

It was David's fourth birthday, and when I reached the corner of Ninety-sixth and Broadway I had a station wagon load of kids on their way back from what was to be their last visit to the old Palisades Amusement Park.

She was lying under the sign "First National City Bank," with blue lips and twitching hands, legs swollen almost to the bursting point. I stopped the car, and two policemen in a squad car drew up in front of me. The four-year-olds continued to play noisily.

What scared me was the fact that she was getting colder and stiffer under the eyes of the small crowd gathered there. Her right hand stopped twitching, and her head lolled about on her neck. She was wearing a pretty blue dress and looked to be around nineteen years old. Her matted blond hair had stopped sweating as I looked, and I actually felt my spirit begin to enter hers.

We picked her up, cops at her ankles, and put her on my front seat. Racing up Amsterdam Avenue to St. Luke's Hospital, I explained to the children in my best mommy voice that everything would be all right; the ice cream was at home waiting for everything to be all right in just a few moments.

We screeched into the emergency exit, and I dashed through glass doors where a pretty blond intern came to my help. A stretcher was rushed out to the car where the four-year-olds had their noses pressed against the rear glass. Following the stretcher, the intern turned to look at me and shrugged.

"We had her here yesterday and the day before that," she told me, almost accusingly. "We can't keep her off the streets, she won't tell us her name or where she lives. No one knows her, and if we can't keep her, we can't treat her. If she tried to kick on her own she would go into convulsions and die."

"Why?" I was screaming silently inside.

"She's on pills and junk," said the pretty blond intern who could have been her sister. "There aren't a hundred beds in the city to detoxify people on pills and junk." She patted my shoulder, leading me out the door.

"It's all right, we'll keep her 'til tonight when she can walk out on her own. It's all right," she smiled at me, "we'll keep her 'til tonight."

Just Hangin' Out, Baby

I was feeling rather pleased with myself. After three months of detailed research and efficient homework and study, I had finally finished a story on the relationship between the crackdown by the federal government on drugs and a rise in the rate of crimes against people. I had compiled figures documenting the correlation between drugs and crime, completed interviews with addicts, pushers, government investigators, and local police, and the whole thing was ready to go. The morning it was to air, I was in the shower with the radio on when I heard President Nixon announce that he had succeeded in lowering the crime rate across the country and had put most of the major drug dealers in jail. The hot water was pouring down my back, and I reached back to turn off the faucet so that I could hear the announcement better. It was like seeing a blind man grope across the tracks while an express train is bearing down on him. I couldn't believe that in half an hour I was scheduled to go on the air and blast the President's statistics out of the ball park—but that's what happened. As soon as I got to my office the secretary called out, "Oh Barbara, the White House called, but they wouldn't leave a name. Can we send them copies of the tapes of your report immediately?" We did.

The story began in late July 1972, when I heard from various street sources that the flow of heroin in the city had suddenly and quite effectively been dried up. A walk through the nearest neighborhood park confirmed the stories. Junkies were sitting around twitching, waiting for suppliers who never came. The talk on the street was that it was the Feds who had finally closed off the supply. A wave of muggings swept New York, and the price of heroin went up twenty percent, while the quality went down until the junk was only thirty-two percent pure. At the same time the previous year heroin had been fifty-one percent pure. I laid out this story like a term paper, outlining all the facts I needed to prove the rumors and making precise lists of every faction with whom I wanted to talk.

I first went to the Police Department and examined their Index of Crime Trends, which showed that crimes against people had risen sharply during the month of July, eighteen and six-tenths percent to be exact, while crimes against property dropped off eleven percent. But during the month of August, street crime was up by thirty-five percent and more in certain precincts. Yet, no one had seen the connection between the rise in crime and the drop in the flow of heroin—or at least no one was talking about it.

After a series of phone calls I finally got an appointment with Andrew Maloney, who headed the federal Office for Drug Abuse Law Enforcement in the northeastern region of the United States. Maloney was a tall, vigorous looking man whose office was located at the end of a maze of other sterile looking offices. He was proud of the way they'd closed down the drug supply and puzzled that I seemed to be the only reporter who knew about it. I asked him how it had been done.

"It was a combination of things," he said leaning back in his chair, "part of it is our program—the program in the Office of Drug Abuse Law Enforcement—and another part is the wide use of the Grand Jury process to disrupt the traffic by bringing conspiracy cases. We also worked with the Bureau of Dangerous Drugs and the Bureau of Customs to make some major seizures over the past twelve months. The Narcotics Division of the Police Department has also been reorganized and given a lot of money to infiltrate and disrupt major drug peddlers." He seemed to be warming to his subject. "The shortage has been going on for close to twelve weeks now. There are always new sources of supply, however, and we're just hoping to keep the lid on."

"How are you going to do that?" I asked.

"Well, we're no longer relying entirely on the classic police undercover purchase of narcotics," he said. "We're subpoenaing suspected drug peddlers and asking the Grand Jury to go into their assets, and if they can't account, we go after them for tax evasion or perjury."

I was so impressed with Mr. Maloney and his straightforward approach that I did something I wouldn't usually do. I gave him the license plate number of a Westport man I knew was pushing a lot of heavy stuff on the West Side. It was kind of a test; I wanted to see what he would do. It's hard to tell what actually did happen. A few months later they rounded up three of the top pushers in that city, but Maloney never said anything to me except "thanks," with a brief nod in passing. It's one of those stories I'll never know the end of.

The next stop in my investigation was the Manhattan north police district which handles—among the other precincts in its jurisdiction—the Times Square area. Patrolman John Tumulty explained to me that during a drug shortage, addicts move in waves uptown seeking new suppliers and a better price.

"That leaves a void in this area," he said, "which is quickly filled by people from downtown who come up knowing there's usually a source of supply somewhere in this area. When this happens the police know to be on the lookout for junkies who have OD'd. They find a pusher who will sell them a five dollar bag that is really the ten dollar bag, because that particular pusher didn't know how to cut it as fine as the previous pusher who had that corner."

Tumulty told me that when the squeeze is on, addicts start closing in on Harlem, where the heroin is usually about eighty-five percent pure.

"The reason is that the source of supply up there is one of the better markets; they must have good stuff. Of course," he boasted, "we can tell when we get one ounce, what country it was processed in, and even in what country the original poppy was grown."

If the addicts were all going to Harlem, I was going too; so I set off, stopping on the way in a needle park—a grassy island in the middle of an avenue where addicts hang out—on One Hundred Sixth Street and Broadway. Two girls were strung out on one of the benches.

"What are you doing?" I began the conversation.

"Just hangin' out baby, just hangin' out." They grinned, swinging their legs and wiping their runny noses on their sleeves.

"Whatcha waiting for?" I asked.

"A drink," one giggled. By this time most of the other junkies had faded away. A blond young man stood around rather conspicuously outside the park next to a car with out-of-town license plates. He, too, seemed to be waiting, pacing up and down and finally circling the park several times. I turned the talk to drugs.

"Any junkies bother you around here?" I asked.

"Oh yeah," they rolled their eyes. "Just the other day, man, I was sittin' here mindin' my business when along come a junkie with some pills and sez does I want some." She rolled her eyes again and pushed up long sweater sleeves to expose track marks on her arms.

"It was only methadone," she sighed, giving me my first clue as to how the panic was being met. "But I ain't on the stuff, you know." She seemed in a hurry to retrace her steps. "We just drink a little, you know. These junkies is terrible. Just the other day I got mugged just for the sweater I was wearin'." She stood up to act out the part. "See, I was wearin' this heavy brown sweater my boyfriend lent me, and this junkie ripped me off just for the sweater."

The effort of explaining all this was too much, and she sort of slumped over on the bench while her girlfriend giggled. I took the opportunity to leave and go uptown to an appointment on One Hundred Twenty-fifth Street with a couple of addicts I knew. They had agreed to talk on film if I'd refer to them as ex-addicts (they didn't want to wind up in jail), but they twitched and sniffled on camera.

"What makes addicts mug people?" I asked one of them, whom I'll call H.

"Well," H. said thoughtfully, "when it comes to the point where, without breaking the law, an addict can't support his habit, his habit gets too big, then he turns to crime, whether it be robbery, stealing from his mother, selling hub caps, stealing cars, mugging; any way that he can get it, that's the way he's gonna do it. He's gotta get the stuff from somewhere, and he doesn't care who's got it, he's gonna get it. And the only way he's gonna stop is if he dies or gets arrested."

His friend chimed in. "But putting a person in jail if he's an addict, it only solves the physical part," he protested. "The mental part is still there and has to be treated. The question of why people become addicts. Most of us think we know why we use drugs, but we don't because we never really look into it."

"Do most addicts have to steal in order to get their money?" I asked quickly, trying to avert a long, drawn out debate on why people become addicted.

H. answered. "Well, most addicts do have to steal in order to get their money, because they're not dependable, they're not motivated enough to keep a job. So they have no other alternative but to steal, because they're not in control of themselves. You don't rule dope; it rules you. It controls you."

"What does it feel like to be out of control?" I asked.

"Believe me, it's a horrible feeling. It seems like all the muscles in your body, they tighten up on you. You start getting running noses, watery eyes, you just, you just become nervous, and you just—you're all in knots, you just have to get that fix."

The two young men I talked with were spending thirty-five to forty dollars a day back then to support their habits. I wonder what ever happened to them.

I was a little embarrassed entering my next port of call —the Twenty-sixth Precinct station house. Twenty million eyes on the block followed me as I went up those steps with my tape recorder. No good reporter with any kind of credibility goes into a Harlem police precinct unless the police are holding a news conference or a special event. But I had previously talked to Sergeant Philip Powers on the phone, and he'd invited me to visit the anti-crime unit and get the lowdown on the drug scene in Harlem.

"The street price of narcotics has tripled," he said, "and where a guy used to have to rip off one person to make his daily supply, he's had to increase his rip-offs on the street to keep up with the cost."

He led me into a room where maps covered the walls. Red, yellow, and blue pin heads marked the locations of anti-crime officers, plainclothesmen who, dressed as hippies and in an assortment of other disguises, attempted to infiltrate the community. They were fairly successful, Powers told me, because they blended right in—they were short and tall, black, white, and oriental, and drove beat-up Fords and Volkswagens.

"Every month this year we've had a decrease in robberies," said Sergeant Powers. It was his job to put a best foot forward.

"Except for what month?" I asked him, looking him straight in the eye.

"Uh, I guess August," he muttered, tracing the graphs on the wall. "We, uh, I guess we attribute it to the tight supply of narcotics on the street." My guess was confirmed.

My research had already shown me that more than fifty-three thousand robberies had been committed in New York City in the first nine months of 1972, and although separate statistics were not kept on muggings, police confirmed the sharp increase in street crime. Assaults rose to 3770 from 2920 of the previous year. Juvenile arrests, drug-related homicides, and other drug-related deaths had also risen sharply in August when the first effects of the squeeze began to show.

A little arithmetic showed me that there were nine murders every two days, upwards of three million dollars in property stolen every day, more than one billion dollars worth of property and cash stolen every year, and over forty thousand arrests made each year in New York City alone.

A few weeks earlier there had been a wave of muggings in the Twenty-sixth Precinct area. What made these muggings different was that they occurred while hundreds of bystanders simply stood by and watched. Sergeant Powers tried to explain this phenomenon.

"Well, I think people would get involved if they thought they could deal on an equal basis," he said. "People have their families to think about, and they're afraid of being stabbed to death and assaulted. But if the mugger didn't have a knife or a gun, they would definitely get involved, I think." He sighed. "You know, we live in a violent society," he said. "People are afraid."

There were one thousand juvenile arrests in the month of August; so when I left the precinct, after chatting with the street-sitters for a while to tell them I was just getting some figures on drug arrests, I moved on to talk with kids in a nearby housing project. I asked the youngsters what they would do if they witnessed a mugging.

"If it was just a regular mugging, just hitting, I guess I would try to help," said one boy. "But if the mugger had a gun or a knife or something, there wouldn't be nothing much I could do."

"Have you ever seen a mugging?" I turned to a little kid of about seven or eight.

"I've seen a mugging once before, down at Morningside, but I couldn't help them because most of the time it's three of them and they have knives, and you know . . ." His voice trailed off. A bigger guy wanted to monopolize the camera.

"Most of the people I know," he said, with a swagger, "they won't bother me. It seems like they only mug people they don't know—you know, people they're not close to or something like that."

"Yeah, they do it to strangers, but they wouldn't want anybody to do it to their mothers or their brothers or any of their relatives," chimed in another young voice.

"Why do you think they mug and steal?" I asked.

The same kid answered. "Well, because they want to buy drugs or, you know, they need it badly. They have to support themselves for the habit of using drugs."

"How old are you?" I asked.

"Eleven."

I talked to close to a hundred people on the streets late that summer, and few adults or children replied that they would go for help or try to stop the crime. Most said that they would run away. That isn't so true these days.

A blind news dealer over on One Hundred Sixteenth Street and St. Nicholas had been held up many times; the most recent robber had placed a knife on his papers and made him touch it.

"I backed up in the corner, and I asked him, 'Why would you want to come here and rob a man like me?' " he whispered from behind his green stand into my microphone. " 'I ain't got nothin'.' So he tells my wife, if I don't do the right thing he will shoot me. And a lot of people

was standing around here, quite a few men, I could hear
them, but nobody, you know, came to my aid. Then somebody musta called the cops. So when the cop came up,
it was two cops, and they talked to him, and then they
asked me, did I want to press charges against him? I told
them, 'No, because I'm a blind man, and I'm afraid that if
I do that I may get hurt.' So they took the guy down to
the corner, One Hundred Seventeenth Street, talked to him
about five minutes and turned him loose. So then he come
back by here and took all my money."

"Was he a junkie?" I asked.

"Yes, he was. I know from his ways and actions and I
could tell by his hand; it was swollen, like from where you
put the needles in."

Most of the police officials I talked with seemed to
think that community involvement is the answer to the
drug problem. Auxiliary or volunteer policemen acting as
the eyes and ears of the community could spot a drug
pusher or a drop within hours. Unfortunately, things don't
quite work this way. Nor is there much help from the 1973
New York State drug law, which gives mandatory life
sentences for pushers; it only has the effect of taking the
addict population out of the jails. Police simply stopped
arresting the user–pusher.

The city's network of methadone maintenance centers
connected to hospitals—originally planned to ease the
pressure on illegal sources of heroin—seemed merely to
make available a lot of black market methadone on the
streets. Methadone, like heroin, is an addictive drug. The
only difference is that it's not addictive in ever-increasing
dosages. A patient can, therefore, be treated at one dosage
level for the rest of his natural life. Methadone is produced
by three major drug firms and is very tightly controlled,

both the shipments and the dispensing of the drug in clinics and hospitals. But nevertheless we were getting reports of huge quantities of "stolen" meth. My street sources reported six to seven hundred methadone tablets or diskets being sold on a single corner, and I suspected that the drug was being manufactured somewhere especially for illegal sale. Robert Nicoloff of the Bureau of Narcotics and Dangerous Drugs disputed this.

"It's just not possible," he protested at first. "In order for pharmaceutical firms to sell raw methadone to anybody, they have to receive order forms from the person to whom they're selling it. And in order for the person to get these order forms, he must be registered with the federal government."

I was curious. "So that whoever is buying the raw methadone from one of the large pharmaceutical companies probably has a drug firm and claims they're using it for some other reason?"

"Yes, but in almost all cases we have found them to be legitimate. There may be slight pilferage going on, but the companies, in and of themselves, are not set up to divert drugs such as methadone into illicit traffic."

"What about illicit laboratories?" I had to check out my information.

"Well, we have in the past come across illegally manufactured methadone in the illicit traffic," he admitted reluctantly, "but we have not come across any legitimate firms selling tremendous quantities." But the tremendous quantities were being sold by the pusher on the street.

"Where would these illicit sources be getting their raw methadone hydrochloride and all the chemical formulas that go into methadone?" I was relentless.

"Oh, I'm not sure. Perhaps by obtaining it under a guise

of being veterinarian-type organizations or some other type of laboratory organization—I just don't really know."

I talked with pharmacists who told me that anyone with a compression machine and a small mixer could make methadone tablets in his living room, but that person would have to have access to the bulk components of the drug, namely the raw methadone. Yet the federal government continued to reiterate that the moment anyone started buying large quantities of these raw products, they would be caught. I continue to insist that the large amounts of methadone still on the street cannot come simply from clinics being ripped off. There are private label drug houses who can indeed buy raw bulk chemicals needed to make the drug. Perhaps they buy it claiming veterinary use or whatever. Or perhaps the corruption that eventually invaded the police narcotics division has also reached the federal people. For in 1973 close to one thousand pounds of heroin "disappeared" from the property clerk's office in police headquarters. Maybe some federal flunky figured out how to duplicate federal order forms for methadone. Whatever the answer, thousands of junkies discovered nirvana in a methadone disket taken just on the peak of a heroin high, and the street price of methadone shot up.

As my reports began to take shape, Maloney's office busted eight hundred and fifty-six pounds of heroin on the East Coast, arresting one hundred and thirty drug dealers in the metropolitan area. They then followed this up with the seizure of another three hundred thousand dollars worth of heroin. At least one part of Nixon's statement about drugs and crime was true: The Feds were waging a war on drugs. But the public was paying the penalty as the number of homicides rose from one hundred and fifty-eight to one hundred and ninety-three in a period of one month, and more muggings took place as bystanders did just that, stand by. I paid another impromptu visit to Andrew Maloney's office downtown, and asked what he hoped to see on the New York drug scene three years later.

"A tripling in size in the Bureau of Narcotics," he replied without hesitation. "More money and manpower made available to the New York City Police Department. I don't think law enforcement can ever wipe out the problem," he was quick to add, "but it can reduce it to manageable terms so that we can at least live with it as a society."

Actually, Maloney's dream has come true at least partially. The addicts were cooled out with treatment programs; there was enough methadone to go around; and the problem was reduced to manageable terms. But what happened to the dream of drug education and preventative programs, the hospital space for barbiturate addicts, large clinics to treat addiction as an illness? Where are the large sums to be spent on a "cure" for heroin? What happens to a dream deferred?

Less than a year later Maloney and his boss both resigned, along with the head of their sister agency, the Office for Drug Abuse Prevention. All had the same complaint: that funds were not being used for treatment programs to prevent drug abuse, but rather to create larger law enforcement agencies. Cracking down on the junkies had not, it seemed, reduced the crime rate; it had, instead, helped to feed an anti-crime industry.

An Easy Place to Serve Time

The Attica prison uprising took everyone by surprise, even those of us who should have known better. For a year or so before it happened I had been getting correspondence from and interviewing a number of people who were behind bars, and so I was aware of the complete turnaround some prisoners were trying to effect in their lives. Blacks and Puerto Ricans in prison were starting to read, study, and teach. The Black Power Movement was late in coming to the prisons; what we saw in the late sixties in prison was simply what had happened to the rest of the country in the early sixties. Yet if Attica happened again tomorrow, it would still take everybody by surprise, for despite all the inquiry commissions and recommendations, the Tombs riots, the killing of George Jackson, and the indictments, the vast majority of people are still totally unaware of what goes on in prison or what the lists of grievances were really all about. They are still ignorant of the way their tax dollars are being spent. It's so much easier not to know.

It was late in 1972 when I began to hear rumors of psychosurgery being performed in prisons, and early in 1973 I began getting horror stories from a place called Dannemora, where one of New York State's maximum security prisons—Clinton Prison—was located. Prisoners charged that they were thrown into solitary, transferred to Dannemora by night, stripped, their belongings taken away; other prisoners wrote long letters about "the hole," a place called Unit 14 in Dannemora where prisoners were kept for weeks on end without water, light, toilets, or adequate food. Shortly after many of the disruptive Attica inmates had been transferred to Dannemora, several legislators had visited the prison and complained that there were no prison reforms in effect at this institution. They charged that Dannemora was a concentration camp.

Just about then Dannemora opened a new wing right next door to the prison, to experiment in something called behavioral modification, and an inmate named Tyrone O'Neal filed suit in a Buffalo court to have the program closed on the grounds that it was unconstitutional. He charged that psychological techniques amounting to "coercive measures of thought control" were being used, and claimed that he had been transferred to the program because he had led a Black Muslim group in his former prison.

I had heard of behavior modification programs in the federal prison system, in Springfield, Missouri, at the Special Treatment and Rehabilitation Training (START) Center, at McNeil Island in Seattle, and in the federal prison at Marion, Illinois. So I called the New York State Department of Corrections, requesting official permission to visit Dannemora and do a story on what I found there. I knew that few reporters had been allowed in, and I was surprised when permission was granted, within a week, for me to tour both the prison and the Adirondack Diagnostic and Treatment Center next door.

I decided to drive up and stay in the town of Plattsburg, near the Canadian border, then travel the ten miles or so to the prison early the next morning. Richard Tomlinson, a courtroom artist, and Doug DiMarco, a young writer, went with me. Before I left, I asked some of my colleagues if I could borrow files of letters from prisoners who feared that psychosurgery was being done. Then I went to see the head of the Fortune Society, an organization that helps ex-convicts and their families.

Their director called in an aide who told me that several prisoners had "disappeared" from the system, and asked me to look for certain names and faces at Dannemora. I had also heard from relatives that prisoners transferred to Dannemora were being held for one to two weeks before being allowed to notify their families of their whereabouts. This report alarmed me more than anything else, since it was a radical departure from standard prison policy in New York State.

We checked into a Plattsburg motel around 10:00 PM and went to dinner. Two girl guitarists and a drummer who sang country tunes were playing to a large audience of college students in the lounge. The kids, laughing heartily over their beers, did a lot to dispel and ease the smell of fear and tension that I knew awaited me the next morning in the prison.

Retiring early, I checked the batteries, AC cord, and cassettes for my tape recorder with special care; I knew that once I was inside the prison, there would be no replacement parts. I also had an extra long cable for going between bars into the cells. We arose at 9:00 AM, and after a light breakfast of eggs and bacon set off for the prison. Nothing we had heard prepared us for the sight of the massive, medieval-looking stone buildings that appeared in the cold gray fog around a bend in the road. We passed the tall stone walls and glass lookout towers, made a U-turn, and stopped, waiting quietly at one side of the road while Richard sketched feverishly. Our visit had begun.

We entered the circular driveway, parked the car, and went down a hall lined with portraits of various renowned individuals to the office of the superintendent of the Adirondack Treatment Center, Eugene LeFebvre. LeFebvre, a tall, dark-haired, rather austere-looking man, did not look either like a jailer or like his descriptions; the most remarkable thing about him was that when you looked into his eyes they were quite flat. He stood behind a long table as he shook my hand and gestured me toward a straight chair. I began with a history of the institution, asking how and why the facility had evolved from Dannemora State Hospital, a facility for the mentally disturbed.

"The hospital was being closed down and the patients transferred downstate," he explained. "Most of the corrections officers here could have lost their jobs. Luckily, many of them were eager to be re-trained to serve in the treatment center. Of course," he added, "I believe the fact that the officers were working partly for mental hygiene and partly for correction was to our advantage—we retrained them in an intensive program, but they were involved in group counseling and intensive therapy before."

I had already learned from inmates and from authorities in Albany that an inmate may be transferred to the center without his consent if he is "recommended" by the warden of his present prison. He is then notified by the State Department of Corrections that he has been so recommended, and has seven days in which to protest; at the end of this time the corrections commissioner can overrule his objections. This process takes time, however, and there were prisoners behind the walls who had been transferred before the initial notice of recommendation ever reached them. So now I asked LeFebvre, "How are inmates chosen to participate in the new program?"

"The inmates' behavior needs are evaluated at other correctional facilities throughout the state, and the evaluation sent into the central office. A central office classification and review committee reviews each individual case, and they make a decision whether the inmate should be sent to our program."

"When you say the basis of behavior, is that behavior in prison or behavior on the outside?" I asked.

"A combination of both." He smiled grimly, the smile never reaching his eyes, and sat back, folding his hands together. I was given a sheet of paper with a brief description of the seven separate programs run at the Adirondack Center, and LeFebvre gave me a ten-minute rundown.

The first program listed was a two-part Diagnostic Treatment Program, a medium security unit fashioned after a drug therapeutic community in which addicts live together and are treated for whatever problems they have; treatment consists of both counseling and peer group pressure.

Then there was the Diagnostic and Treatment Phase III program, an incentive-type behavior modification minimum security unit; the Stress Assessment medium security center for inmates having a history of violent crimes; the Community Preparation Program prepared inmates to live acceptably in the outside world; and the Adult Correctional Camp, a minimum security unit where inmates performed daily work, mostly in forests, outside the prison.

Dannemora also served as the Northeast Reception Center for all prisoners entering the State prison system. Here, in maximum security, they underwent diagnostic evaluation, orientation, and classification, before being moved to a permanent prison. The last program listed was the prescription unit, or Rx Correctional Program Unit. The sheet said: "This outfit aims to perform diagnostic evaluation and develop individual prescription programs for the entire state-wide prescription correctional and control programs." I asked LeFebvre what this meant in layman's terms.

"They take men who had been 'troublesome' in prison, and design individual programs for them to return to in another prison," he explained.

"Troublesome in what way?" I persisted.

"Well, you know, troublemakers." That grim smile again. "Some are murderers and the like; others have just been violent in jail, you know, ready to start trouble." He rose quickly, signaling an end to our interview, and we all went down the hall escorted by the aide, who had been standing attentively by. We were introduced to Peter Lacey, a tall, lean, blond man who was head of the Rx program, and several other program directors, all of whom would accompany us on the tour. The directors, neatly attired in dark suits and ties, led the way downstairs, through a maze of long, sterile underground hallways, to the inmates' area. Most of the doors were freshly painted in bright colors, and, as we went, our guides explained that inmates and guards had worked together to finish the construction and renovation of the building.

We came to a large room with stone walls where several

men in fatigues were playing cards. This was the Stress Assessment Center, for those prisoners with a history of violent crimes. We were told that we could talk to any inmate who wanted to talk to us. Doug and Richard fanned out, Richard sketching faces furiously, Doug with a second tape recorder, talking to the men lounging around in the community room. Jessie Barnes, an older man with a scarred face, looked up from his cards as I asked what the institution was doing to assess his particular stress.

"They can do it by various methods," he began. "One would be aversion treatment, you know, and environmental control. Any time you place individuals in a certain environment they have a tendency to adapt right according to that environment." He was being very cagey. "If you're under maximum security all your actions would be different than if you were under minimum security." That was all he would say, but several other inmates were signaling to me wildly with their eyes and eyebrows that he was uncool. They silently pointed to another, younger man, and I strolled over to talk to him.

"I came to the Center because I was curious," said the second inmate. "We had heard various things about lobotomy, and the various psychotherapeutic methods that they employed here." He shook his head puzzlingly. "I didn't know what level it would be on, and it was a brand new program and no one seemed to know what was happening." He shrugged and smiled at the guards.

"What's happened to you since you've been here?" I said, lowering my voice so that only he could hear me.

"Well, actually nothing." He seemed concerned. "It's just a waiting process; the program's relatively new, you know."

"Have you seen a psychologist?" I asked.

"Not yet; I haven't seen anyone."

"How long have you been here?"

"Uh, about a week."

Surprisingly enough, even though the Center was a few months old, most of the prisoners had only been there from two to three weeks. Many complained that the program was only on paper, that after being given a battery of psychological tests, nothing at all had happened.

I wasn't given much time to mull over what I saw in the Stress Assessment Center before we were led off on the next leg of our tour by Robert Lacey, who kept up a running commentary on the prison program as we walked. When we passed a small, barred, closet-sized door with a heavy steel chain and lock, Lacey explained that this was his baby—the prescription program, which designs a program for each inmate that will help him stay out of trouble when he is sent back to his regular prison.

I asked if we could go in and look around, since I wanted to make sure that Tyrone O'Neal was alive and well; he had been returned to the prescription unit after bringing suit in Buffalo, and had not even been present at the last courtroom hearing on his suit against the prison.

But Lacey flatly refused us admission, saying he could not be responsible for our safety. I made a scene, demanding that they call the State authorities in Albany. One of the men went off, returning five minutes later to report that Albany had told them to use their own judgment; a statement which I later found to be untrue. I don't think they made the call at all. At any rate, there was no way I was going to get anywhere near that Rx program or the dozen or so inmates inside. The closest I got was an introduction to a man who Lacey claimed was the only inmate who had already graduated from the Rx program. Jerry

Bray was a young man who talked a lot, shifting his eyes.
I asked how he had been brought into the program.

"I had some trouble in Elmira—you know, fighting,
fighting with officers—so I was in the guardhouse. They
came one day and told me I was leaving. I said I wanted
to know where I was going at, but they didn't tell me, so
I refused to leave. So they brought a whole lot of officers
over there, and I went. They didn't tell me where we was
going 'til we got all the way up here, then they told me
I was going to Dannemora. . . . They put us up there in
Unit 14, which was a box. I stayed there for about a month
up there, and then I went back to my cell. So I came one
day from the shower, and I seen they had all my stuff
packed up, they said I was goin' to the program, you know,
over here." He frowned. "But I thought it was still like
they said they had it once before, where they give you all
those pills and try to mess you up and everything. But
they said now it was nothin' like that. As soon as I got
over here, they let me make a phone call and . . ."

"Who'd you call?" I asked.

"I called my people, my father."

"Where's your father?"

"In the Bronx."

I asked Jerry Bray what happened when he got to the
Rx program.

"Well, I stayed in the cell for a month, until they finished taking all kinds of tests and everything. After you
take the tests, then you come out of the cell, and they have
an upstairs where you go to a room and live. You've got
the room. You have to go out of the room just to go to the
bathroom or the shower room. You stay out 'til nine at
night." Jerry said that all the time he was in the prescription program he only saw other inmates' backs, coming

and going. Most of this time was spent in his cell, where he wrote poetry and did push-ups. Two to three times a week he was given a series of tests, which I was later told were the standardized personality tests, the Tennessee Self Concept Test, the Berner–Gestalt, the NMPI, and in selected cases, where the co-operation of the inmate was available, the Rorschach.

"Did they give you any drugs at all?" I asked.

"No. Uh-uh. None at all."

"Well, then what happened after they diagnosed you?"

"Well, I started staying out 'til nine. Mostly we ended up with nothing to do, so what I did is play chess all day. From there I just came over here to the Community Preparation, where they prepare us for parole."

"How did you get out of the Rx program? Why did they tell you you were ready to leave?" I probed.

"They said that I passed and everything. They said that there was no need for me to stay over there any longer."

I couldn't figure out whether he was a ringer, or whether anything at all was going on.

"What criteria were they using to say you passed?"

"I think this whole thing is mostly for people who don't want to get along with the system. So this is why they got these programs for us, figuring that when we see these programs have got different things right here, we'll take another step up."

"You're saying that you acted all right?"

"They must have thought I did."

"In what way?"

Suddenly Bray seemed to connect with what I was saying. "Quick to jump at them. That's what they don't like. I wasn't no model at first. At first . . . if they say something out of the way to me, I would hit one of them, see."

He closed up again, just as suddenly, and we moved on.

We walked through another series of corridors in the labyrinth to a large room that had smaller rooms opening off it. Here I was told that I could talk with the prisoners alone in one of the small rooms if I wished. Only one guard stood near the entrance to this section, next to some curved iron bars.

The first inmate I talked to grinned and said everything was just fine, just fine, but the next prisoner, a short, wiry young man with coal black skin, walked boldly into the room and asked for Richard and Doug to leave. I gestured them out. He told me furiously that he had been brought to Dannemora against his will.

"The first and foremost thing I want to do is to leave here," he said, in clipped tones, his hands darting about as he spoke. "This is a ball of confusion."

"Do you want to go back to your other prison?" I asked.

"I have no qualms about going back behind the wall," he answered, "because I had more freedom." He had, he explained, been taking courses at Auburn Community College while in Auburn Prison; when he got to Dannemora he was told he'd have to wait eight months before he could continue his studies.

"But," he pointed out, "the law provides that an inmate can go to school if he has one year or less until parole."

"When is your parole coming up?" I asked.

"My parole comes up in October. These people circumvent the law whenever they choose to. The law means nothing to them."

"What are you in for, and what was your sentence?"

"Possession of a forged instrument."

"What is that?"

"Fraudulent papers—might be negotiable bonds, checks, et cetera," he explained.

"How much time did you draw?"

"Well, I've been here for twenty months out of a three-year sentence, but I have another sentence which extends past the three years."

"And what was that for?"

"Seven years for robbery."

"Oh." I was silent, but he pressed on the attack.

"One of the most atrocious things that they are doing here is in Unit 3," he said. "They have an individual by the name of Dr. Ron Green who wrote his thesis on co-optation, and if you are aware of any of the concepts of behavior modification, it's just a flowery, verbose word for brainwashing." There seemed to be nothing I could say to that.

We passed on, from one big, newly-painted room to the next, stopping briefly in the library, a large room with only a few books and unpacked boxes of film cartridges on its brand-new shelves. Throughout the Center inmates wandered around, for the most part gaping at us. I asked one of the few white inmates, a tall, sandy-haired man of about thirty-five whose name was Tom Higgins, if he had been given any drugs, or any kind of mind-altering chemicals while in the Center.

"No," he replied, "the only drugs I take is for epilepsy."

I later found out that there is a disproportionate number of epileptics in behavior modification programs, and that there has been an ongoing experiment funded by the Justice Department at Boston Hospital where psychosurgery has been performed specifically on epileptics. The operation is known as amygdalotomy, and the surgeons say they operate only on patients with temporal lobe

epilepsy and would never operate on patients with a normally functioning brain. What I wondered about as I
walked through Dannemora was whether inmates with disruptive histories are assumed to have normally functioning brains, or not. It wasn't a question I could answer, and
it would take a team of doctors living inside one of these
behavior modification programs several months to determine exactly what, if anything, is actually being done to
the inmates.

As we approached the noon hour, it became evident
that I couldn't visit all seven, or rather six, of the programs. My guides asked what I specifically wanted to see,
so I asked to visit Dr. Green's program called Unit 3.

"Ah yes . . ." was the response and we were led into
another huge room that would have seemed dungeon-like
without the bright paint on the walls and doors. More than
a dozen inmates were hearing a huge, beefy "counselor"
explain the system of punishment and reward that the
Center used. "The way you move, from one level of priv-
ilege to another is by earning points in the program," he
told them. He had the air of a kindly father explaining the
facts of life to eleven overgrown sons. "Now, if ya keep
your area clean or go to bed early, that may be forty
points. You spend these points by staying up for a late
movie or going to the commissary." The men sat, trying
very hard to comprehend. One or two asked questions or
joked and tried to look eager. It all reminded me of my
first day in second grade when I knew that no matter how
good I could possibly ever be, I would still have ten years
of schooling to go.

The group broke up after ten or fifteen minutes and I
went to interview Dr. Green in a room with glass windows

on two sides. Apparently you could see out of this room but not in, because it was several minutes and much confusion before Richard and Doug could find me again, although I could see them all the time.

Dr. Green was a young man who had just gotten his PhD in experimental psychology and behavior modification from the University of Vermont. For three years, while in school, he had worked part time at Dannemora State Hospital. One of his teachers had been Dr. Stewart Agras, a behaviorist whose approach to psychiatric problems was to change behavior rather than to deal with the root causes of such problems. Dr. Green described his prison program at Dannemora as an application of the principles of B. F. Skinner in community living. He described these principles briefly as the positive reinforcement of socially acceptable behavior.

"Behaviors that are followed by pleasant or reinforcing events tend to be increased in frequency," he told me, polishing his glasses. "Those that are followed by unpleasant events tend to be decreased in frequency."

"How do you select subjects to test these principles?" I wanted to know.

"For our program we require that a man be between the ages of twenty-one and thirty, relatively young by institutional standards. Although we would prefer that he have a long history of delinquency, we prefer that he not have a long history of State incarceration, to the extent that he might have become institutionalized. We also require that he be between six and eighteen months away from eligible release. Although the board in Albany that selects prisoners for the program doesn't have to meet my criteria, they've been co-operative so far."

I asked Green about psychosurgery.

"Under no circumstances are we doing any surgery in this institution," he replied sharply.

"What about hypnosis or chemotherapy?" I was probing in the dark.

"We're not using either of those. At one time, when this institution was Dannemora State Hospital there was extensive use of chemotherapy for the mentally ill, but under its new structure we're not using chemotherapy, other than as an occasional anti-anxiety agent." I wondered about a passage I had seen in the program manual which read as follows: "A fine core of basic services are provided for all programs. These include a Medical Service with a 25-bed infirmary which provides diagnostic services, preventative services, and treatment for all but major illnesses. Capabilities for X-ray, laboratory studies, electroencephalography and electrocardiography are provided. There is 24-hour medical coverage." Was I, perhaps, seeing shadows where there were none? Perhaps the inmates' fears of surgery are created by the fact that the facility was formerly a mental hospital. Perhaps they stem from the very real fact that a large hospital with two fully staffed operating rooms lies just on the other side of the wall in Clinton Prison. The warden there later told me that he does treat patients from the Adirondack Center, but only for plastic surgery and "anything they can't handle." He was quick to add that any case of major surgery would have to be sent to a public hospital.

The last inmate, with whom I talked alone in an unsupervised interview, pooh-poohed the rumors about the program on the grounds that nothing at all was happening, either good or bad.

"There are just men here filling up space. There are no

programs available. They have them on paper, but in actuality the programs don't really exist. They just transfer men from different institutions and put them here to represent a program."

"What do you do all day?" I asked.

"I have school in the morning; in the afternoon I work in the laundry."

"How much do you get for working in the laundry?"

"Twenty-five cents a day. That's one of the real beefs of the program. This is supposed to be community preparation. All the fellows here are getting ready to get out. And most of them that come from other prisons where they're in jobs learning trades, were making a lot more money than they're making now. They're taken out of the prison, brought here, and given twenty-five cents a day. You aren't learning any trades, you aren't getting any skills, and they're telling you that they're preparing you to go back to the people, which is ridiculous!" He shook his head and walked away.

Doug, Richard, and I were shown back to the front building by another circuitous underground route. There, when I said I was going on to visit Clinton Prison next door, there was a hearty laugh all around. But they would only say that I'd find a big difference.

The first difference I noted was a feeling of traveling backwards in time. In the two minutes it took us to back down the nicely paved driveway and into the muddy parking lot at the other prison, it was like going back forty years. The first thing I noticed was the forty-foot stone wall, with glass guard towers on top and a small gate cut into the side of the stone. The rifles, electric gates, and turrets peeping over the wall all prepared me for the metal detector we had to go through.

The artist and I cleared all right after removing our loose change, but our production assistant Doug was put through time after time, with the guard behind the glass window shaking his head ominously after every trip. Doug removed his watch, then a heavy metal belt, and the bell kept ringing. Finally, much to my relief, they nodded him on, never finding out what was causing the detector's alarm to ring. Doug later realized it had been the metal pin sewn into his leg because of a war injury.

After being escorted past some of the most hostile-looking guards I have ever seen in any prison, we were ushered into an empty office filled with pictures of horses, and we sat down to wait for the prison's superintendent, J. Edwin LeValle.

As we sat, I reviewed in my mind what I knew of this man. Among those legislators who had been highly critical of the whole Dannemora complex was Assemblyman Arthur Eve, a friend of mine who was one of the negotiators at Attica. I had spoken with him by phone a week earlier and he had charged that large numbers of prisoners were still being kept in solitary, solely because they spoke out on social and political issues. He said the superintendent at Clinton Prison was probably one of the worst within a state penal institution.

"This is the same warden who said to me that he locked forty-one men up because he considered them revolutionaries," he had said, his voice crackling with anger over the phone. "And when I asked what do you mean revolutionaries—how do you tell one?—he said 'I tell by his writing *right on* at the end of his letters.' "

Suddenly, the man I had been thinking about walked in, a tall, heavy man with beadlike eyes, and I was aware of that peculiar kind of horror that comes to a reporter when you find yourself face to face with a legend of whom you know you are going to have to ask some very hard questions.

"We have a good program here," he said, in a deep, drawling voice. "Only a hundred or a hundred and fifty prisoners out of the general population of sixteen hundred eighty-five men are idle." I noticed that on his blackboard he had broken the population down by racial designation (something rarely done in prison administration these days). I wanted to meet these statistics in person and asked to interview some inmates. The superintendent gestured to the yard and said, "Go ahead. There they are."

One corrections officer accompanied us past the six-story cell blocks through a corridor and out into the yard, where there were some twelve hundred inmates. Guards with rifles stood in twenty or more elevated huts scattered throughout the yard, and the loudspeaker kept calling for different groups to fall into line. The yard looked more like a French vineyard than a jail, with several "courts" landscaped in tiers climbing up the hill. A few men were working out with weights, but most just stood around talking quietly in small groups. I was surprised at the large number of Spanish-speaking inmates and the few whites.

When we entered, a slight ripple went through the prison yard, but not even a whisper was spoken. There is a kind of silent language in prison. No one dared to come over, or even to show surprise. I stood there for a full five minutes, mike in hand, just sending them signals that I was cool. There is a silent language in our business too. Then I started to interview the corrections officer who'd come out with us, just to tell the guys that I was a reporter.

The officer told me that when an inmate is assigned to a "court," he is the manager, totally responsible for that court, and can have other friends of his on the court with him.

"Prisoners are allowed in the yard for approximately one hour each day, idle inmates for two, and most of the day on weekends," he explained. "They cook; they play all different types of card games. They have gardens; they grow flowers. And almost, as they say themselves, they try to make it a home away from home."

After we had been in the yard for ten minutes or more, during which Richard was impressing them with his drawings and Doug was rapping with a few prisoners, I stepped up to one group and asked if they would talk to me. In the meantime Doug had managed to whisper to me that several guys had told him they were afraid of reprisals if they talked to me. So I stepped in close, extending my mike the full length of my hand, and blocking the guard with my left shoulder until there was no way he could have heard our conversation. But he certainly did try.

"What's happened to you? How long have you been in here?" I didn't know where to start.

"Oh, I've been down pretty close to thirty months now," answered one inmate.

"What's been your experience here?"

"Huh?" I could see myself getting nowhere fast.

"How often do you get outside?" I asked.

"Outside where?"

"Outside in the yard."

"I come out every day."

"For how long?"

"Twenty minutes, an hour, something like that."

"When do you come up for parole?"

"I be maxing out." This means serving the full time.

"What do you hope to do? Have you had any help in finding a job?"

"Huh?"

"Have you had any help from the facility in finding a job?" At this point I think he finally realized the guard couldn't hear a word.

"No, this place don't give you nothin'. Don't give you nothing'."

"What do you expect?" I asked.

"From here? Nothin'."

"How has it been?"

"Ugh! What can you say, it's a jail. Any jail's a jail."

"No worse than any other jail you've been in?" I asked.

"Well, it's kind of bad, very bad," he said surreptitiously.

"In what way."

"It's ancient, you know. I'm tired of being locked up. Everybody is I guess."

Another inmate stepped up boldly.

"I just got here," he said.

"Where did you come from?"

"Sing Sing."

"How was it there? Is there a difference in the prison?"

"No, not necessarily," he shrugged. "Maybe it's a difference in the clientele, you know, officers, that's all." There was a laugh all around. "As far as inmates, no."

"What about the officers? How are they different?"

He laughed. "You don't really want me to answer that do you?" The other inmates crowed. "Take five, man, say you take five," they chanted.

"Yes, I would like you to answer it," I replied.

"I'll take five. I'll take five on that."

"OK," I smiled, shaking in my boots, eyes glued to the trained rifles on top of the walls.

"Is there any rehabilitation going on?" I asked another black inmate, who looked like a young child.

"No."

"None whatsoever?"

"No," he replied. "I mean, how can you rehabilitate a man in an institution that doesn't have anything rehabilitating to offer? You know, as far as rehabilitation is concerned, it's something that an individual has to do himself, because they ain't got it here."

The officer prodded my elbow, signaling that it was time to move on to a Catholic chapel high on the hill dominating the prison yard. We went through a locked and chained gate in a barbed wire fence, up a hillside of slippery, icy steps, and found ourselves in a small court with a fountain. The guard explained that the chapel had been built in 1940 with inmate labor. The wood on the altar originally came from Magellan's ship, and he said proudly that it was the finest church building anywhere in the vicinity. He seemed to unbend as he told me that the church was presently being used by the clergy and their staff to visit with inmates and their relatives, and to hold services on Sundays. At any rate, the only pleasant look I ever saw on the guard's face was when he was talking about the church.

As we passed through the yard on the way down I asked if it would be possible to talk with certain specific prisoners. Their names included Martin Sostre, the famous Buffalo bookstore owner, and Felix Huerta and Bill Codigan, many of whose letters I had read only a few days earlier. They all told of subhuman conditions in the box at Clinton.

"Would they be in the yard?" I asked innocently.

He asked for a written list of the names and quickly disappeared with it into the building. After less than five minutes he returned, saying that those men were not available. He took us back to the warden's office, where once more I asked about these men. LeValle reminded me politely that I had asked only to talk with men in general, not to specific individuals. Under no conditions would I be allowed to visit Unit 14, the segregation unit. Even if I could see these men, he told me, "who knows whether they'd want to see you. Many of these men write out to the newspapers, but when reporters arrive they don't actually want to talk. Take Martin Sostre, for example. You don't know how many reporters call here asking to talk to him, but he won't see a single one of them. Just keeps to himself. Do you have any more names?"

Instinct told me to discontinue this line of conversation as fast as possible. But I had to ask if Sostre was in Unit 14.

"I couldn't tell you that." He smiled benignly, closing the conversation—but I had more questions. Prisoners in Unit 14 claimed that they were being beaten and placed in cages with no showers or toilets, and that their slop pails are sometimes removed for days at a time. Because of the large numbers of reports of brutality on the part of the guards, I asked the superintendent point blank if there was truth in these accusations. He made the distinction between brutality and physical force.

"I don't think there's any violence. I don't think there's any need for fear of reprisal," he said. "The men, the staff and the population are familiar with the laws and rules and regulations."

"Are you confident that your correction officers are not brutal to the inmates?"

"There's no doubt in my mind about whether they are or not," he replied. "I know they're not. I'm positive of this because in any case where physical force is essential and is used, the first thing we do is attempt to gain control by a show of strength, a show of numbers." LeValle said that as far as rehabilitation is concerned, the most important kind is physical rehabilitation, hospitalization or exercise, and he went on to describe the modern miracles of plastic surgery, disease cures, and internal medicine that went on in his hospital, of which he seemed proud.

"Rehabilitation is a word that means an awful lot. Maybe the first thought and the easiest one to talk about is physical rehabilitation," he said thoughtfully. "Maybe a man has got a harelip or a cleft palate or a crippled hand, or something of this nature. Or he has a disease of some kind that's curable. Whenever anyone comes in, any inmate that arrives here goes through an orientation period, and he's interviewed by psychiatrists, psychologists, counselors, and various boards. He's examined physically. As a result of this experience, we try to develop a program for the individual, the one best suited to his individual needs in terms of what we have available."

When I asked the superintendent what, if he could, he would change at Clinton, he said he was perfectly happy with his staff, which was adequate. He would ask only for a gymnasium, an all-faith chapel, and a new school building. He said his dream was for a chapel where all religions could worship on Sundays, not only Catholics.

We talked about why, although more than three fourths of the prisoners at Clinton were black and Puerto Rican, the warden has had trouble attracting non-white guards.

"We have three Puerto Rican correctional officers who speak English or are bilingual, and they work with the Puerto Ricans or any group, but especially with the Puerto Ricans," he explained. "Blacks, we haven't been able to get. There's an intensive recruitment program going on to try to get minority groups, but as yet they don't like our climate, or they . . . just something they don't like about the place. I think it's the atmosphere, the climate."

"Does it get pretty cold up here?" I still can't believe I asked that question.

He looked me straight in the eye. "Sometimes, yes." It wasn't too cold on the day I was there, although there was snow on the ground, but I didn't like the atmosphere either. The guards were hostile in contrast to those next door, and a stern, almost military sort of discipline was in effect. The stone corridors were dark and dank, and everywhere prisoners had seemed sullen and idle. But LeValle's office was still sunny, although it was growing late. We stood up to leave, and LeValle and his deputy showed us out. We shook hands, and LeValle looked at me almost kindly.

"Dannemora is an easy place to serve time," he said. "If a man wants to try, the opportunities are there."

At the gatehouse twelve or fourteen guards crowded behind us into a small glassed-in room where exit passes were collected. The doors at either end of the room were locked, and the guards played a game of counting how many of them could squeeze in before they slammed the door. Laughing now, the cold air steaming from their nostrils, they waited until a lieutenant was almost there, calling "Come on, Lieutenant, hurry up," only to clang the gate cruelly in his face as he was about to take that last step inside. The glass walls echoed raucous laughter as the lieutenant waited patiently on the doorstep for the next group to pass through the small glass room and out into freedom.

Glory Be

It was the middle of November when a strange story appeared in a local newspaper: glowing images of crosses had been appearing in the bathroom window of a woman's apartment up in the South Bronx. The story was sufficiently weird that my editor decided I should investigate it—and so I took a train to the South Bronx, walked a few blocks, and finally found the apartment. It would have been difficult to miss—a line of people were waiting outside in the hall to get in.

Mrs. Viola Mitchell, a small, pleasant-looking black woman in her mid-forties answered my knock.

"Come in, come in," she said, gesturing me into a small, somewhat shabby-looking living room. "Please stand aside, the Press is here," she informed her neighbors.

Leading me into a tiny but immaculate bathroom, she

told me to stand up on the toilet seat. I did so, feeling foolish but skeptical; and I discovered that even though there was no light hitting the window or the vacant lot under the window, there were three images of the double cross, the cross of Lorraine, blazing brightly back at me.

"Hmmmm." I stalled for time. "Turn out the bathroom light." Her eyes shone brightly up at me from the dark. I looked again—the crosses were still there. "What's causing it?" I wanted to know. Mrs. Mitchell turned the light on again.

"I don't know," she said, helping me down, "but the crosses suddenly appeared three days after my son Anthony got married. His wife's expecting a baby now you know."

I didn't, so I went back to the living room and met the rest of Mrs. Mitchell's family, which included a barking dog and an eleven-year-old son. A neighbor who had been standing in the line outside the front door emerged now from the bathroom, shaking her head.

"I feel those crosses are out there for a very good and definite reason," she announced, wagging a finger at me. "It has been several strange incidents happening in this community since the crosses was here."

"Such as what?" I challenged her.

"Oh, a horrible, hideous thing took place. A little infant found dead in the yard opposite the cross. According to some, the mother is supposed to have placed the body of it there, brought it out and laid it in the backyard."

"That same night a teen-ager was also killed nearby while trying to prevent a gang fight," chimed in Mrs. Mitchell. These two occurrences are not uncommon in the South Bronx—certainly not uncommon enough to make a story—so I nodded and thanked everybody and was about to start back to the station when the central character made her entrance. Stringy blond wig askew over a coal black face, Mrs. Marcella Monroe was all skin and bones. She introduced herself as a clairvoyant with a New York State Baptist minister's certificate.

"But I've learned to harness my clairvoyance," she explained, frowning slightly at my presence. I sat down on a plastic-covered sofa and stared at her, mesmerized by her strange speech patterns.

Since the image of the crosses had appeared in the bathroom window two weeks earlier, Mrs. Monroe told us, she had been a daily visitor.

"My apartment was robbed a few weeks ago," she began, in what seemed a non-stop stream of conversation. "So I went to bed one night after I left here and . . . well, I don't know whether I was really asleep or not, when the burglar's image came in front of me, and then I became really aware of myself, you know. I couldn't remember right then just who this person was that I actually saw, and then within myself a voice says to me 'your things are in a two-and-a-half room apartment.' " I struggled to keep a straight face.

Mrs. Monroe explained how she had gone to the police and led them to the apartment house across the street, where they found her TV set and arrested the young man whom she claims to have seen in her dream. "It's the crosses; it's a sign," she said. I nodded, suitably impressed.

"In Texas last week," she went on, "there were ants raining from the sky all over cars. And the man that reported it was afraid to even call or tell anybody. He didn't want anybody to think that he was losing his mind. His car was loaded with ants or spiders, and some laboratory tested the webs of them and said it was like angel hair.

All the cars was loaded with spiders," she said wonderingly, fluttering her bright red nails. "I really don't know what to think."

"Could the reflection be in the glass itself?" I asked, turning the subject back to the crosses. Mrs. Monroe spoke authoritatively.

"If this had something to do with the glass, I feel surely after all these years it would have already appeared." She had a point.

"The crosses first appeared in Georgia, where I have relatives," said Mrs. Mitchell. "Why here and now? What's going to happen?" she wondered.

During our conversation a couple of Baptist ministers had come in and out of the bathroom, and there was a steady stream of neighbors who had come by after work, carrying shopping bags and worn purses, mouthing "glory be."

"Some people been coming here, you know, wanting to give me donations," said Mrs. Mitchell, "but I refused them, you know, refused to let it touch my hand. I say to them if they want to place it any place in my home, I'll send the donations to my church in Georgia."

I went back to take one last look at the crosses, which were still reflected in the dark glass. I opened the window on the November dusk—there was no street lamp shining on the vacant lot under the window. I thanked Mrs. Mitchell, and in parting I asked how it had felt over the last two weeks to live with a cross in her window.

"I feel good to live with it. I'm not afraid," she said, smiling for the first time. "If they should go away I would feel a sense of loss, you know. I'd wonder what happened all of a sudden." Mrs. Monroe, settling herself in a comfortable chair for the rest of the evening, nodded wisely.

Outside I ran into Mrs. Mitchell's son playing handball against a lobby wall with a group of his friends.

"What do you think the crosses mean?" I asked them.

"Oh," said one kid nonchalantly, "it's just the end of the world!"

Back at the station I made a few calls. The Associated Press in Texas reported that there had been an overfertility of spiders in Mexico whose cobwebs had been blown across the border, resulting in a "rain of angel hair" in Corpus Christi. The owner of the Brunswick Glass Company in Georgia told the sheriff that one brand of his glass did indeed contain an interior pattern of vertical and horizontal lines which just might produce special effects. Later that night, vandals smashed the lower pane of Mrs. Mitchell's bathroom window, and the crosses appeared in the upper half. I did a few pieces on the strange story and then put it out of my mind, going on to my next assignment.

But when I went to work the next day, dozens of people took me aside—rather shamefacedly to be sure—asking, "Did you see it? Was it really there? A cross? What did it look like? What does it mean?" There were executives, salesmen, accountants, and secretaries, all hoping, believing in spite of themselves, that something special had really happened.

EPILOGUE

It is midnight, and I am sitting in front of an open window in my friend's study in Connecticut. As I work I hear small noises, the dogs moving around, rabbits playing on the lawn and the wind blowing through the tall swaying pine trees that surround the house. An hour earlier, a car circled the drive, apparently lost, the occupants hidden by darkness. The Merritt Parkway is just down the hill, and I can hear the steady rush of cars speeding by. But up here it is quiet and dangerous. As I work I glance up in thought, and each time I can see bands of howling figures advancing on the pine grove, trying door knobs and finding them open. I look through the window into darkness, seeing families of Charles Mansons who creep softly, ready to draw blood and wake all the sleeping children in the house.

I see crosses burning brightly on front lawns, white sheets disappearing through the underbrush.

I work slowly, a page at a time, thinking only of my work. But each time I glance up, there is the open window, which I know is, for my friends who live there, only a means to see out. For me it is a danger point, a solid obstacle standing between me and the outside world, an object with a dimension of its own.

I think of the tomatoes and lettuce growing off to one side of the window, try to frame it with the turned-off sprinkler and still swaying swing hanging from a tree. But it is no use. I begin to smell hatred and fear advancing on me, and eventually I must get up and draw the blinds.

Back at home I work all night with all the windows open, stopping only twice to call the police to comfort two separate mugging cases, the perpetrators of which have long since disappeared into the neon void down Broadway.